ISRAEL

—THE INGATHERING—

GOES ON

Esther Lever
With Russell Bowles

Published by Sovereign World Ltd
Ellel Grange
Bay Horse
Lancaster
Lancashire LA2 0HN

www.sovereignworld.com
Twitter: @sovereignworld
Facebook: www.facebook.com/sovereignworld

Previously published by Zaccmedia.com

ISBN 978-1-85240-817-6 (Printed edition)
E-Book 978-1-85240-827-5 (Kindle edition)

Printed in Great Britain by Bell and Bain Ltd, Glasgow

Dedication

I dedicate this book:

Firstly, and most importantly, to the Lord Jesus who never leaves
me and is always there beside me. Without Him I can do nothing
of any worth.

To my beloved children who have patiently put up with
their mother travelling to faraway places, often not knowing what
I am doing or when I'll be back.

To my dearly loved grandchildren, now grown up, and my
precious great-grandchildren – surely a gift from the Lord.

Contents

Acknowledgements

I wish to express my deepest thanks to the following people whom the Lord has sent my way to help me in writing this book:

To Russell Bowles for assisting me in writing the book, especially when he has been extra busy with his family.

To Peter Barraclough for his capable proofreading.

To the "family" of Ebenezer for allowing me the privilege of participating in their work of bringing home the Jewish people.

To my dear friend "Hannah" for her patience and wonderful partnership when we travelled together as a team.

To all the many prayer partners who have constantly supported me with prayer, love and sacrificial giving, enabling me to go wherever the Lord sends me.

To the Elim Church of Risborough, where I am a member, for their love, encouragement and support at all times, meeting my needs for prayer cover, transport, checking my home when I was away and in many other ways being there for me.

To dear faithful Marilyn Shepherd who still sends out my newsletters, often at short notice and at her own expense. She has done this for over 30 years! Her carefully kept record of these letters has been an invaluable help in writing these stories.

Foreword

Fishing for Jews! This might sound unusual, unless one remembers the words of Jesus: "Follow Me, and I will make you fishers of men" (Matthew 4:19). But nonetheless, fishing for Jews? Yes, for Jeremiah the Jewish prophet prophesied nearly 3,000 years ago:

> *"I am going to send for many fishermen," declares the Lord, "and they will fish for them; and afterwards I shall send for many hunters, and they will hunt them from every mountain and every hill and from the clefts of the rocks."*
>
> (Jeremiah 16:16)

This book is not only about the fishing adventures of Esther Lever, as she seeks out the Jews of the East, and those from Central Asia as well as those from the ends of the earth. It bears testimony to God's heart and to His faithfulness to His Word, in regathering His scattered people Israel, who have been dispersed to the four corners of the world (Jeremiah 31:10). The adventures that Esther shares with us in this, her second book, will encourage and challenge each one of us as to what it means to be a fisher of men as an obedient servant of the Lord.

Time and again we will see how God sovereignly arranges for Esther to find and then meet with Jewish people and to share with them a simple message of hope that their God, the God of Abraham, Isaac and Jacob, the Father of our Lord Jesus, has not forgotten them and that He is calling them home to their land, the land of Israel, given to them by the Lord God and eternally secured by His everlasting covenant. This return is known in Hebrew as the *aliyah*. God's purpose in returning the Jews to the land of Israel is that that they might receive the revelation – given to us as Gentiles – that Yeshua (Jesus) is Israel's Messiah and be brought back into the covenant relationship (Ezekiel 36:24–32; Zechariah 12:10).

It is not widely known, but since 1948 over 3 million Jews, from over 100 countries, speaking 27 different languages, have returned home to the land of Israel. Dear reader, the meaning of this is clear. We are living in days when the prophetic utterances of the prophets are being fulfilled before our very eyes, that is, if we have eyes to see! We are moving closer to the end of this present age and to the return to this earth of our Lord Jesus.

It is a joy to know Esther personally. She is one of those Christian disciples whose life is a testimony to what it means to be led by the Spirit of God. Esther was present at the beginning of "Ebenezer Operation Exodus" in 1991, a wonderful ministry, founded by Gustav Scheller. Esther's path, while not leading to the birth of a significant end-time ministry, has nonetheless run parallel with that of Gustav. The reader will recognize that she shares the same kind of pioneering spirit.

Ken Hepworth, 2015
International Bible teacher and author

Preface

Since the publication of my first book, *The Ingathering of Israel*, many people have been asking me to produce another. I realized that there were still many trips to recount and exciting stories to be retold, and so I decided to heed their requests and embark on the writing of this second and final book.

I can say that I have been privileged to travel to many parts of the world in fulfilment of God's calling on my life. He has continued to do amazing and often miraculous things without which I could not have completed anything that He led me to do. It is God Himself who put the plans together and God Himself who completes and accomplishes everything. I can do nothing of any worth without Him. He is behind this great ingathering of the Jewish people which is continuing daily. He will go on doing it because, in His Word, He says He will do it, with or without us, because it is for the glory of His Holy Name (Ezekiel 36:22).

In between some of the trips described in this book, I visited countries where there proved to be no Jewish people, just places to pray – such as North Korea, Vietnam and Cambodia. In other countries, such as those in Africa like Nigeria, Kenya and Tanzania, my visits, while being to places where I could teach in the churches, brought me in contact with only a few Jewish people. The story was different, however, in Ethiopia, where Israel was at that time taking groups home each month. Other journeys by train have been for prayer purposes in order to reverse the curses on routes to the Nazi Holocaust camps. This prayer action would effectively open highways for the Jewish people to go to Israel from the nations of Europe – from Poland, the Czech Republic, Slovakia and Hungary, and from Germany, Austria and Italy.

In the year that the Berlin Wall came down (1989) there was also a long journey in three stages, a prayer journey when I really learned to listen in detail to the Lord's instructions. For two sections of this journey, Helen Mears, of the ministry "Streams in the Desert", travelled with me. I also went with her as a prayer partner to visit Jewish people in Ukraine, who were potential elderly *olim* (immigrants to the Holy Land) for the homes she was establishing in Israel. Other trips included taking seven prayer journeys to Israel, four times serving as a civilian volunteer with the Israeli Defence Forces (IDF), and frequently going into Ukraine with my elder daughter, working with street children and the elderly Jewish people in Dneprodzerzhinsk. None of these trips involved "fishing" (searching for Jews) and just a few gave me opportunity for teaching in churches. For this reason, the stories, although generally exciting, are not included in this book. But my experience has shown me how the Lord will use us in many ways, if we are willing and available. It makes life very exciting. Who ever dares to say being a Christian is boring?

One really special journey which I will mention briefly was when four of us were led by the Lord to pray around South America for a move of God on the Jewish people to "make aliyah", i.e. immigrate to Israel. We went to the far south, to the island called Tierra del Fuego – Land of Fire. We stayed in Ushuaia, the most southern city in the world (where it snowed in September). From here we took a catamaran out towards the Antarctic, to the southern-most lighthouse in the world. There we blew the *shofar* (ancient Jewish "trumpet" made from a ram's horn) and proclaimed Scriptures relating to the return of the Jewish people from the ends of the earth. Surely this was an "end of the earth"! We also prayed along the Amazon River, from where the tributaries join to form the beginning of the river at Manaus, for a long way downstream – a highway to the open sea. A big treat was seeing green river-dolphins jumping up in the water. It truly was a special journey. Our mandate was to pray for the Jewish people to return to Israel, not to find them, although there are many there. In all, we travelled from Buenos Aires down to the south of Argentina, across to Tierra del Fuego, back and across by bus to Chile and north to Santiago. From here we went to Lima in Peru, on to Caracas in Venezuela, and south to Manaus in Brazil. Then lastly we travelled east to the coast in Recife and then down to Rio de Janeiro. This was all done in a month and could almost make a book of its own.

So I hope you enjoy this book and recognize how much the Lord's Hand is on this current ingathering of the Jewish people. Maybe you are already in a group praying for Israel and/or the aliyah, but if not, I do recommend being involved, praying for what God is doing and becoming a small part of it.

1

A Strange Place For Fishing –
Tibet

"Behold, I am going to send for many fishermen," declares the Lord, "and they will fish for them; and afterwards I shall send for many hunters, and they will hunt them from every mountain and every hill and from the clefts of the rocks."

(Jeremiah 16:16)

It was January 1991. The annual Prayer Conference organized by Ebenezer Operation Exodus in Jerusalem had just begun. There were 120 delegates from 24 nations. There would have been more but many had cancelled their bookings and some airlines had stopped flights to Israel because of the threat of war with Iraq. Saddam Hussein had invaded Kuwait and threatened war with Israel if the US-led coalition attacked. His Scud missiles could reach Israel without difficulty and there was a great fear that he would use chemical weapons or gas, which he had threatened.

In Jerusalem we had been equipped with gas masks and the hotel had provided rooms that were sealed against gas attack by covering the windows with plastic sheeting. Every private home was told to set up such a room.

During our second night at the hotel we were woken by sirens. It reminded me of my childhood during the Second World War. Grabbing our gas masks we all made our way to our appointed "sealed

1

room". Once everyone was inside, the doorframes were covered with brown sticky tape. We all followed instructions, putting on our gas masks and laughing at the way we looked. We couldn't speak but at least we could pray. It was hot and uncomfortable, with the masks smelling of rubber. And the time seemed to pass very slowly. Two hours went by before we were told we could come out. This happened every night, but during the day the conference proceeded normally. There was complete unity among those who were present and a lot of intercession.

It was during this time that Gustav Scheller had the distinct impression that the Lord was telling him it was time to start bringing Jewish people back to the land that God had given them. He shared this with the other leaders and they felt it was from the Lord. Gustav then told the rest of us and explained that he would need a lot of help and finance for such a venture.

As Gustav shared with us, I sensed the Lord speaking softly to me: "This is what I want you to do: go and help him."

After the meeting I went to Gustav and said to him, "The Lord is saying I am to help you."

He replied, "Oh no, I haven't got you to add to my troubles!"

I wasn't sure then whether he was serious or joking. Had I misheard? Had the Lord really said I was to help? In my heart I knew He had.

The Gulf War, as it came to be known, lasted for six weeks and ended just as the Jewish festival of Purim was beginning. We got used to the sirens and even the bother of carrying our gas masks everywhere.

There was a great unity among the people in Israel, whether Jew or Arab, foreigner or local. They had a common enemy and they helped each other in a remarkable way. Israelis can be pushy and noisy, especially in queues, but suddenly a care for one another blossomed overnight, which was wonderful.

Sometimes I would be seen carrying my Bible and would soon have a crowd around me. "What is God saying?" people wanted to know. "Has He told you anything?" It was strange to be surrounded by people I hadn't met before, asking me such things, and I read out comforting passages to try and encourage them. One amazing thing was that every day in Israel at that time the newspaper headlines featured Scriptures! To my knowledge this has never been seen in Britain or America.

It seemed to me to be very significant that the war ended at the start of Purim when Jews all over the world celebrate their deliverance from the evil schemes of Haman, as told in the biblical Book of Esther.

Saddam Hussein had also wanted to destroy the Jews but it was clear that God was watching over His people. After the war, accounts of amazing escapes emerged which could not have been anything but miraculous. A baby was buried in the rubble of a building but the masonry had fallen in such a way that it had cocooned her and she was found asleep but unharmed in her little protective shelter called a mamat in Hebrew. Another family were unable to get into their air-raid shelter because they'd lost the key. They stayed indoors and a Scud missile took the roof off the shelter where they would have been hiding! There were many such stories. In all, 39 Scud missiles were fired at Israel and there was only one fatality. There was significant cause for an especially joyous Purim that year!

~

In the spring of 1992 I had a clear impression that God wanted me to leave Israel. I knew that He had called me to work with Gustav Scheller assisting in the aliyah, but now I sensed a temporary change of direction. It was as if God was saying that first I needed to go to Tibet! Tibet was unlike anywhere I had been before and seemed so remote. In the past I had had a feeling that I would go there one day, but it seemed that God was saying now was the time.

As I mulled it all over in my mind, I became rather concerned that I would miss out on my calling to help Gustav and imagined that

3

he would have brought out all the Jews in Russia by the time I joined him. What a foolish thought that was! God is never wrong and I should have realized that. He impressed upon me the facts. There were about 2–3 million Jews in the former Soviet Union. If Gustav brought out 500 each week, that would be 24,000 in a year! So how long would it take to bring out 3 million? I got the point and laughed.

Why go to *Tibet though?* I thought. Was there a Jewish community there? If there was, it could surely only be small. If I contacted them what else would I do?

After much prayer, to be sure of the Lord's leading, it became clear that my friend Hannah and I should go together. It was our first of such journeys and we found we needed to go through Nepal to Tibet and then Hannah would return home to care for her elderly mother, while I would continue on across China to Outer Mongolia and make my way back through Russia and Ukraine.

A friend had done this journey a year or so before and was a big help with advice. Hannah also was far more experienced at this kind of travel than I was.

As we waited on the Lord for guidance it became clear that, apart from looking for Jewish people, we would be doing some spiritual warfare in various places and taking financial help to Christians, because it was difficult to get their support to missionaries in these countries.

Katmandu

On May 3rd Hannah and I flew from London to Karachi via Dubai. In Karachi we changed to a smaller plane for our flight to Katmandu in Nepal. We flew over the foothills of the Himalayas, catching glimpses of snow-capped peaks among the stars as it became dark.

Upon landing in Katmandu we were taken to the Shangri La Hotel. It was a little oasis of calm in a frenetic city. Traffic was chaotic as there was neither a right nor a left lane, so old cars, buses, rickshaws, people and animals (especially cows) jostled for a place on the crowded roads into whatever side seemed best for them at the time. Compared to Western standards the roads were rather narrow and, needless to say, progress in whatever direction was of a necessity rather slow and accompanied by much tooting of vehicle horns.

On the sidewalks in front of the small shops people sat making things for sale, or repairing things using whatever tools and machines were necessary. The air was filled with the whirr of sewing machines which seemed to be the favourite item. Bare-footed small children played among them, wearing nothing but a cotton vest, oblivious of passers-by.

In those days Nepal was a Hindu country and Christianity was not encouraged. However, there were missionaries working as doctors or agricultural advisors, and their supporters in the UK had given us money to pass on to them.

A brave man had a Christian bookshop. This was wonderful as Hannah and I had felt led by the Lord to pack some Bibles in our luggage and we were able to give some to this man.

At every opportunity, of course, we enquired if there were any Jews in the city. People told us different stories. Some said there were none and others said there were many, but we found they were referring to Jewish people serving in the Israeli Embassy. The shop owner selling the Bibles said he knew a man who he suspected was Jewish, but who pretended to be a Muslim. He said he would make enquiries for us.

~

The next morning we were having a leisurely breakfast in the garden of the hotel while a troop of monkeys entertained us with their antics on the hotel roof, chattering and chasing each other.

This peaceful idyll was suddenly interrupted – I had a telephone message. Who could this be? No one knew we were here. The message itself was also cryptic: "Reggie will meet you at 12.00 noon in reception." It quickly dawned on us that this might be our Jewish contact. We rushed upstairs to our room to pray for the meeting and prepare some Scriptures to give him.

At 12.00 noon, the reception area was crowded but we recognized "our man", not only by his olive skin but by his dark curly hair – the Himalayan people had straight hair. We invited him to come and have a drink of cool juice in the beautiful garden of the hotel.

The poor man was totally mystified why two ladies from England would want to see him. My first words were quite direct: "You are Jewish, aren't you?" He paused, thinking carefully about what I'd said, and then replied that he was indeed Jewish. We were thrilled. We told him that God had sent us to find him and that He was calling the Jewish people to return to the land promised them long ago. He was absolutely dumbfounded as we showed him Scriptures from Psalm 139 confirming that God knows exactly where we are. From other places in the Bible, we showed him how God is today bringing His people back to their Promised Land. He was amazed, silent at first, but eventually began to tell us his story.

His family had fled from Yemen many years before, due to trouble there, and his grandfather, who had been a rabbi, brought them to Calcutta. However, the climate didn't suit them, so Reggie's father moved the family up to Nepal where it was cooler. Here Reggie had grown up and now had a Nepalese wife and two children, David and Esther. His sister had a Nepalese husband and three children. They were the only Jews in Nepal.

We asked Reggie if he wanted to go to Israel. He said that he did and had actually tried once, unsuccessfully, so had given up. We encouraged him to try again, telling him as much about Israel as we could and we gave him the Scripture verses we had prepared. It really was a God-given time. He told us his business address so we could find him again and we parted, promising to call at his office.

After this exciting encounter, Hannah and I went to visit the Israeli Embassy. How difficult it was to get into the building! It was the most securely guarded of any I have visited. Eventually, after passing through many security checks, we were allowed inside. It was just as if we were in Israel with pictures and maps and Jewish things. The consul was a delightful man who made us very welcome. We told him how we, as Christians, loved the Jews and were seeking them out to encourage them to immigrate to Israel or "make aliyah", as they themselves call it.

"Oh, but there are no Jews in Nepal," he said. A silence fell and he must have twigged that we knew differently because he said, "Or are there?"

We told him about Reggie and his sister and their families. The consul was amazed, especially when we told him how we had found Reggie. He had been unaware of them. We gave him Reggie's address and parted, hoping that the consul would follow up the contact and that Reggie would eventually get to Israel.

~

During our exploration of Katmandu we found a hidden church in a house where one of the elders had an amazing testimony. He was a witch doctor before conversion and had been paralysed in his legs. Someone had prayed for him and the Lord had healed him, resulting in his giving his heart to Jesus.

The efforts of the church to spread the gospel in their city were seriously hampered by the simple fact that 90% of the population were not able to read. Giving out any form of literature was clearly going to be a waste of time and resources. We were told of another way that was effective in these situations and that was to show people a video film which explained the message of Christ. However, the lady pastor, who actually came from Tibet, could only hire the equipment periodically due to the cost.

Hannah and I both had the same prompting of the Spirit that we should buy the church their own television and video player. We each had some money back in England and felt that it would be a fitting and proper use of some of it to assist this church in their gospel outreach in this way.

We crossed town in a rickshaw and found a retailer that accepted credit cards. This was amazing as in Katmandu they were hardly known. The sum of £500 procured the equipment that was needed and we took it back to the church in a "taxi", which was a hair-raising trip! The pastor was overwhelmed, really delighted, and so were we.

Small gifts of $50 each were given to various believers as we felt led of the Holy Spirit. One such deserving case was a man who had rescued ten small boys whom he found living in some derelict shacks down by the river. He put five to lodge with his mother and the other five with his sister, providing for them as best he could from his small salary as well as caring for his own wife and two children. They really were such precious people.

Through the Himalayas

While we were in Katmandu we had applied for visas to enter China and at last these came through. Tibet, although in the past independent, was part of China and we needed Chinese visas if we were to travel to Lhasa, the capital.

A bus with 20 people aboard picked us up for the journey and it wasn't long before we found out that many were Western Buddhists, unfriendly and uncommunicative, going to Lhasa. A few were Christians really going for the excitement of the trip.

The Nepalese countryside was lush and beautiful, full of green valleys bordered by hillsides terraced with rice paddies and small houses. As the bus climbed higher we gradually left these behind and then down we went again to the Chinese border, which turned out to be across a bridge. The customs officials were sitting under a tarpaulin as it was raining heavily. The Bibles in our luggage might prove a problem. We believed we should bring them so would have to trust the Lord with this. If they were discovered we could be in trouble. We had been given a customs form to fill in but I had left blank the section enquiring about books. We were standing outside waiting our turn to see the officials, heavy drops of rain running down our faces. At last it was my turn.

"Literature?" the official asked.

"Oh," I said, "you mean my book." I showed him the book I was reading and he flicked through it. There were no pictures and he passed it back seemingly unimpressed, indicating that I could go. Hannah was treated in a similar way. Hallelujah, we were through! However, many of our travelling companions were searched thoroughly and had books taken off them. The officials were looking for materials about the Dalai Lama which were perceived as anti-Communist.

Back on the bus we wound our way higher and higher to a primitive village where we would stay the night. To say that it had running water would be truthful: it ran down the centre of the road and found the easiest route downhill. Wooden houses in the local style clung to any convenient space on the rocky slopes. How long they had been there was difficult to judge but they looked pretty old, which brought some comfort as they must have been reasonably secure!

During the night there were heavy storms with the result that one side of the road that we needed to drive on was washed away. Our start was delayed while it was rebuilt and we were told that we wouldn't be leaving until 5.00 p.m. This meant that it would be dark and there would be no chance of seeing Mt Everest. Disappointed, we spent our time walking around the village, praying that God would hasten the repairs to the road. Suddenly we were recalled and incredibly the bus left at 1.15 p.m. instead!

The road was only the width of the bus, and the gaps in the side of the road had been filled with earth and were therefore less firm than they should have been. As we drove uphill the driver told us all to lean against the right-hand side of the bus which was next to the mountain wall. By doing this the wheels on the left-hand side were raised just enough not to make the edge crumble away!

Naturally speaking, this was a hair-raising journey, but amazingly both Hannah and I had peace in our hearts. God had told us to make this journey and He had a purpose for it. This did not include being killed in a bus accident so we trusted Him, and the bus made it safely to the better road at the top of the hill.

Higher and higher we went, grey mists dampening the surroundings and revealing here and there monstrous peaks that reminded us that we were in the Himalayas. Where was the one we wanted to see, though? Everest seemed to be doing her best to stay hidden.

Suddenly, and only for a few seconds at a time, the grey mists would part and there she was, raising her head higher than all the others – and then gone. It was awesome to glimpse this giant peak way above all the others. My family would want to see a photo so I tried to take one, but it was difficult.

The gearbox of the bus groaned and strained as it climbed higher, eventually dropping us off at our "hotel". The hotels all seemed to be the same up in the mountains – dark because there were no lights; and the water, if there was any, was always cold.

It seemed the bed linen in these places was never changed. Hannah and I turned the sheets over and the duvet covers inside out, but probably many before us had done the same thing. We could not be fussy so made the best of it, sleeping fully clothed and using torches when light was needed.

Breakfasts consisted mostly of a warm steamed roll with some kind of green or brown vegetable leaf – exactly which kind we couldn't tell. During the day at least we got some spicy rice and cold drinks when the bus stopped at villages.

Several of our overnight stops had strange names, but we couldn't tell if there was anything unusual about these villages because it was always dark. It seemed there was always a power cut!

Our route took us up through two of the highest mountain passes on earth. Everything got damper and greyer the higher we went, and it was in the high but more level places that we came across tattered Buddhist prayer flags fluttering mournfully in the wind.

We had brought with us our own spiritual symbol that the Lord had shown us – little yellow flags with Scripture references relating to the Lordship of Jesus written on them. Here and there were heaps of large stones in piles, and the Holy Spirit impressed upon us that we should place our flags among these stones. We had to do this very carefully, for our Buddhist travelling companions would not have appreciated our meddling.

The rarefied atmosphere at this altitude was beginning to take its toll on our breathing, and even when we had started to descend to our next "hotel" we were still affected. We found it difficult to carry our cases up to our room and had strange pains in our necks.

~

Sitting in the bus the next day as we descended, we saw the landscape change to one that could more be called "countryside" as opposed to rocky slopes. We came to wide flat-bottomed valleys with the mountains far across each side.

We were on the Katmandu–Lhasa Highway, but it was really just a dirt road cut through the mountains, twisting and winding, full of potholes and in places ploughing straight through riverbeds which thankfully were dry at this time of year. No McDonalds or Happy Eaters here; not even any toilets. Comfort stops meant men on one side and women on the other, with the bus for privacy in between.

Now lower down, we had another problem – Tibetan children. If the bus stopped so that we could take in the view, they would flock around us crying, "*Mimmi, Mimmi*", whatever that meant, hoping that we would give them something. They were ragged little souls, their garments often tied with string. Their faces bore sore patches from the wind and their hands were filthy and their noses runny. If any of us gave them food, they would scramble for it, fighting each other for every crumb. The other passengers would give them photos of the Dalai Lama which the children grabbed. Whether this was out of true appreciation or because they grabbed anything that was offered we couldn't tell. Sometimes even adults would appear saying, "Dalai Lama, Dalai Lama", eagerly grabbing the pictures.

A while later we came across villages where there were Buddhist temples. We were taken to see them as part of the tour. The Chinese had set this up to convince tourists that religion was free in Tibet but really this was a lie, for hundreds of followers had been murdered and the remainder were still persecuted. It was in these places that we realized we should scatter our seed pearls.

When we were preparing for the journey, God had shown us to take with us some tiny pearls that are used in embroidery. They're called "seed pearls". We didn't know why, but we felt they would perform a symbolic function during times of prayer and spiritual warfare.

We looked round the temples and noticed very young boys, dressed in the maroon robes of Buddhist monks, with their heads shaved, sitting cross-legged, studying books, while dogs with dreadful skin conditions lay around in the sun. It was very sad to see these children like this.

As we walked through the living quarters, singing praises to the Lord, we declared His Lordship over the place and scattered the little seed pearls as we did so. Amazingly the monks did not seem to mind. Whether they knew what we were singing we couldn't tell, but they smiled encouragingly and seemed pleased.

In one village temple, up some steep steps, there was a particularly large and grotesque statue of Buddha that had snakes depicted around his neck. In front of the steps a man was prostrating himself as an act of worship.

For some reason I knew that I should go up the steps to the statue. It wasn't something I would normally have wanted to do but I knew I was being guided by the Holy Spirit. Equally Hannah knew she was not to go up to it.

I got to the statue, in front of which was a place to throw money, and there were yak-wax candles burning, giving off a pungent smell. I walked from one end to the other, praying and scattering the "pearls". When I reached the end I could just about see along the side of the statue where it was dimly lit. Suddenly a voice said in a cultured Oxford accent, "It's all right, you can come round here. Just come." I couldn't see anyone but knew I should go round to the rear of the statue. As I went to the back the voice continued to reassure me and so I prayed the Lordship of Jesus over the place and scattered the "pearls".

When I reached the other side I looked for the person with the Oxford accent but there was no one there, just our group going back down the steps.

While I had been at the top of the steps and round the back of the Buddha, Hannah had been busy at the bottom, also praying and scattering "pearls". We felt sure the Lord had got us to pray for a reason and that He had done something special in this area of spiritual darkness.

As we left, one of the monks, who could speak some English, questioned me about Christianity. What an opportunity! Hannah covered me in prayer as I only had a few minutes and briefly outlined the gospel message. He told me he could get a New Testament and that he would read it to learn more. How wonderful! It seemed a confirmation of the spiritual warfare we had been doing.

Lhasa

Eventually our bus reached Lhasa and a good hotel with hot running water. At last we could have our clothes properly laundered! We had not met any Jews or Christians so far in Tibet. What were we to do? Hannah and I sought the Lord about it and felt we should look in the market place, but how could we get there when we had to stay with the group?

We were obliged the next day to take a full tour of the city. First we went to the Potala Palace which had been bombed by the Chinese when they had invaded Tibet. Many monks had been murdered and others driven away. Strangely enough the palace was now being repaired by the Chinese to make it a tourist attraction.

Everywhere we went, women selling cheap souvenirs pestered us, even while we sat having an ice-cream in a park at lunchtime.

The tour next included a visit to another temple. Where? In the market place! As the bus drew up, Hannah and I were the first off – and there, yet again, were the women with their souvenirs. Here the road was made of huge dark rounded stones, and dear Hannah, turning from these women, fell heavily on one side. We all helped her up but she was obviously hurt. I sat with her at a convenient place while the guide, not particularly concerned, left us and took the rest of the party into the temple.

After a time, Hannah insisted she was well enough to walk round, but I could tell she was in quite a bit of pain. For a long time we looked at the stalls selling all manner of strange wares and wondered how we would find any Jewish people. I prayed to the Lord to send us a sign. Seconds later, a man called out to us. I think he saw that Hannah was tired and struggling and that we were very hot. He invited us to sit under his awning where he was selling sweets. He was very friendly so we pretended to sell his goods.

I suddenly felt that the Holy Spirit was drawing my attention to three men at the next stall to my left. They were selling cloth. Excitedly I realized that one of them, unlike almost all other men in Tibet, had curly dark hair and hairy arms.

Using mime, I tried to ask them if they were Chinese. There was a negative response. I tried asking if they were Nepalese or Indian and even used the Russian word for Muslim. Still the same negative shaking of their heads. I then tried asking if they were Jewish, Hebrew or Yiddish. Sadly this didn't produce anything positive either. Then with a streak of inspiration I said "*Yerushalayim*" (Jerusalem), "Israel?" They suddenly went off like fire crackers, jumping up and down shouting a strange word, "*Ammo, Ammo*", and banging their chests. This wonderful response began to draw a crowd, no doubt to see if they were missing anything.

Hannah had joined me and together we showed the three men some postcards from Jerusalem. They looked at them with great excitement and wonder.

Using mime we managed to ask basic questions about their marital status and children, and even if they wanted to go to Israel. They seemed to understand. We gave them Stars of David made of olive wood which we had brought with us. We had to show them to put them around their necks as they thought they were earrings!

In all the excitement, I forgot to take a photograph of them. I did manage to get an address from one of the men, who knew about five words of English, and tried writing to him when we got back to England. However, sometime later the letter was returned to me with the note, "Insufficient Address"; so we just have to trust that the Lord will cause the seed we had sown to germinate in His time.

~

Back at our hotel we looked at Hannah's arm and, fearing it was broken, consulted a Chinese doctor, who assured us it wasn't. However, it transpired that he was wrong because back in the UK she had it X-rayed and sure enough it turned out to be broken badly.

I am, even today, amazed at her courage, for she didn't complain although I am sure she did not sleep that night. She just allowed me to make a sling for her arm out of a scarf and continued as if it was not too bad. It was certainly an attack of Satan, but later we realized that the Lord had used the situation to direct us to the Jewish men in the market.

We flew to Chendu where we stayed one night and there we parted. It was the hardest thing to leave Hannah to go on to Hong Kong and the UK alone. The Chinese doctor had said her arm was not broken. How wrong he turned out to be!

I felt convinced I should go on to China and travelled back overland through Russia, which was quite an adventure in itself.

2

A Journey Home through China, Russia and Europe

Be strong and courageous! Do not tremble or be dismayed, for the Lord your God is with you wherever you go.

(Joshua 1:9)

I parted from Hannah and was escorted by an official to the airport, from where I flew to Chongqing, a damp, misty place with rats running in the streets. One day there was enough!

It seemed that the tourist system in China worked in a similar way to that in the former Soviet Union (fSU). In other words, tourists were not trusted and were watched and escorted at all times. If you contacted anyone, they were interviewed to find out why; so you had to be very careful. It was the anniversary of the Tiananmen Square massacre and security was very tight.

I didn't know anyone and the Lord had impressed upon me that I should not try to contact people but just pray in the places that He showed me. He seemed closer to me now, even though I felt alone after leaving Hannah.

Down the Yangtse River

From Chongqing I took a boat along the Yangtse River to Wuhan. The boat was basic and crammed to the gunwales with passengers.

There were about a thousand people on board and there weren't many cabins. Most people just found a space to sleep wherever they could on the deck or in the gangways. Thankfully I had a cabin but I shared it with three other women and four men, two of whom were soldiers. Apart from the eight humans it was occupied by a large cockroach about four inches long that ran across the wall by my bunk. Fortunately one of the soldiers caught it and threw it into the river. I prayed there wouldn't be any more.

The journey down the Yangtse took three days and I would often sit on a stool in the entrance of the cabin as the boat was so crowded. Many people would come past and say, "Good morning, speak English?" no matter what time of day or night it was. It was all they knew. They were very friendly, so different from the scowling faces of those who had lived under Soviet Communism.

I had no food with me and this seemed to be a concern to my cabin mates. However, I did have some powdered tea with which to make a hot drink. One man wanted to taste it. He kept saying, "Corfee, Corfee?" assuming that it was coffee.

There was a large flask of hot water in the cabin which someone refilled whenever necessary. My cabin mates made themselves a fresh jar of tea each morning, throwing the remains from the previous day into the river. The fresh leaves were then topped up with water on and off all day.

The voyage took us through a well-known beauty spot of three gorges, but the beauty eluded us as the scene was shrouded in mist as we went through. The river, too, wasn't attractive at this point, being a thick suspension of brown mud.

We stopped regularly at small towns where, as on a train journey, some passengers would get off and new ones would get on.

Late afternoon on the first day a wonderful aroma of food filled the air. Exploring, I found that there was a "restaurant" where one could get a hot dish with rice served in cardboard bowls with chopsticks. To get there meant "climbing" over other passengers who were installed along the gangways and stairs.

Bringing the food back, I realized, would be tricky as I would have to come the same way without spilling any on the people. Outside the "restaurant", however, I found an area of seating that was crowded with people. Graciously some of them cleared a whole table for me to sit down and eat. They then watched closely to see if I would leave any! Every so often one of them would emit an "Ooh" or an "Aah", indicating that it was good food and obviously would be good for them too. I knew this was the case as the friend who had done the journey the year before had told me to leave them some! I intended to do so.

The meal was somewhat less than appetizing, being lumps of fat in gravy with some rice. I managed to pour some of the gravy over the rice and ate a little but left most of it. I smiled encouragingly at my would-be guests and went back to my cabin. I saw that politely no one touched it until I had left. They were such dear people and most of them had very little of this world's goods. Unfortunately I had no way of communicating anything of the love of God to them. I couldn't tell whether any of them were Christians and certainly none of them looked Jewish. I just had to leave it with the Lord and pray. The next day I had a lot of abdominal pain and an upset tummy, so for the rest of the journey I ate nothing.

Early on the third day my boat ride down the Yangtse terminated at Wuhan and I was put in a luxurious hotel right on the river. Here the Lord led me to pray over the city from the bridges and the high towers.

~

I then flew to Xian, home of the famous "Terracotta Soldiers", which had been recently discovered. I was taken to see them on a standard, very basic Chinese bus, which was another adventure, as no one spoke English!

When I saw the grey, clay soldiers in ranks of five, a chill went through my body and I found myself praying in tongues as there was such a demonic presence.

I learned that the emperor of the time had had these life-size replicas made of his own army and then had the actual soldiers buried alive after his death! He himself was buried with a huge chariot and horses, also of clay. It was a remarkable piece of work, but although I prayed, I found it hard to shake off the feeling of death. I was glad when we left and returned to Xian.

Beijing

The next stop was Beijing from where I was to book my flight from Ulan Bator in Outer Mongolia to Moscow. However, the airline insisted there were no seats left and said the best thing to do would be to try again when I reached Ulan Bator. However, they were sure there would not be a cancellation. On the other hand I felt sure there *would*, because the Lord had given me that particular date.

I was going to travel to Mongolia by train but there was something greatly concerning me. I had some money that I needed to give to some missionaries in Mongolia as well as instructions to buy them some food. However, somewhere during my travel I had lost their contact details. How was I going to find them? I was alone, didn't speak the language and had no telephone number or address. All I could do was pray and ask the Lord to sort it out somehow.

As I left the travel agent's office I asked the Lord what I should do and I felt that I should go to Tiananmen Square, the site of a terrible atrocity the year before when Chinese troops opened fire on a crowd of unarmed students. It's huge with a mausoleum at one end containing the body of Mao Tse-tung, the famous leader of Communist China. In the centre, Russian style, is a huge memorial commemorating those deemed "Heroes of the Revolution". Along the sides are little gardens and at one end across a busy highway is the Forbidden City, home of a former emperor and now a tourist attraction.

Thinking I was to pray in the square, I took a few steps into it and immediately pains shot up through my legs. This seemed to happen whenever I walked in places where Jewish people had been murdered in the Holocaust. I wondered why it was happening here. God spoke to my heart: "The blood of Abel is crying out to Me." I realized how filled with pain the Lord was at the murder of the protesting students a year before. All they had wanted was more freedom. The government had mercilessly sent tanks and soldiers to quell the demonstration, killing many and arresting hundreds. What happened to many of those detained, no one knows. It was certainly a place to pray.

I felt that I should take Communion in the square and had a miniature bottle of wine that I had been given on one of my flights. However, I had no bread, just some biscuits. Should I do it now?

No, the Lord indicated to me that I should wait. Not sure why, but knowing there was always a reason when the Lord showed me something, I wandered across to the Forbidden City, which was not yet open. However, there was a little market close by, where I bought a Chinese ice-cream and prayed quietly while I walked around.

At precisely 10.45 a.m. I felt the Lord was saying to go back to the square but walk along the left-hand side. I obeyed and halfway down felt compelled to turn right and walk to the huge memorial in the centre. It seemed to me that I should sit down at the front left-hand corner. Two ladies were there praying, heads bowed, and one of them held a can of soft drink. I could see they were British and, not wanting to disturb them, walked past. Immediately, though, I felt as if a hand turned me around to go back to them. They looked up and I said to them, "I think I am here to do what you are doing."

They replied, "We are taking Communion. We have bread but no wine, hence the soft drink."

"I have wine but no bread, only biscuits," I said. At this they invited me to join them. We took Communion and prayed individually about the situation in China.

Afterwards they quizzed me about what I was doing in China. I told them where I'd been and that next I was going by train to Mongolia but had lost the address I needed.

"We have just come from Mongolia," they said. "We've been there for three weeks with ..." and they named the *very people* that I needed to find! How I rejoiced. God had done it. I'd asked Him to solve this problem and He had. How amazing that it happened like this. It showed me again that if I was willing to follow His instructions there was no problem God couldn't solve.

I told the ladies about the problem and we laughed and laughed together at what the Lord had done. It seemed so amazing!

They told me they were from the north of England and we arranged to have a meal together before I left for Mongolia. I have kept in touch with them ever since.

~

While in Beijing I felt that the Lord wanted me to go to the Great Wall and pray there. It is somewhat of an idol to the Chinese and I felt that the Lord wanted me to read Scripture verses from Genesis, chapter 1, how God created the world, and Psalm 24 that "The earth is the Lord's ..." and to proclaim over the wall that Jesus Christ is Lord.

I booked the visit with a tour group, but when we were there they didn't seem to take any notice of what I was doing and what I was praying out loud over the wall, so that worked out all right.

I did not meet any Christians but sometimes I would catch a glance from someone, and the Holy Spirit in them witnessed with the Holy Spirit in me and we both knew we were believers. Of course, though, we couldn't say anything to each other for the sake of their safety. I didn't meet any Jews this time, though much later on another trip I did, but that is another story!

Into Mongolia

The very next day I caught my train that was to take me on the 36-hour journey to Ulan Bator, capital of Mongolia.

My compartment had four bunks, but after I was settled, six men came in with bundles of goods wrapped in sackcloth; mostly clothes, shoes and toys. They were black-market traders of some sort and apparently had bribed the woman in charge of the carriage, for they had one ticket between them.

The idea was that they would sell their wares from the train windows at each station when they reached Russia. The bundles of goods filled the centre of the compartment right up to the ceiling – and I was stuck! Throughout the journey the men sat on the bunk edges, including mine, playing cards and drinking, throwing the empty bottles out of the window with no regard for safety. Needless to say, I had little sleep.

As the journey progressed it became clear that the men were quite friendly and even shared with me a greasy strip of meat they were eating. Years later, to my horror, I discovered it was cat! With sign language and a little Russian I tried to talk to them about the Lord as I felt there must be some purpose in my being with them.

When we arrived in Ulan Bator they signed to me to wait while they unloaded their goods, ready for another train. Then one of them took me to hail a taxi. He threatened the driver, warning him not to overcharge me, and I realized it was the Lord's way of looking after me. The poor driver was visibly shaken, but he soon found the address of the missionaries given me by the ladies in Beijing and they were overjoyed to receive the money and food I had brought.

Mongolia at that time was in the grip of a food shortage because the Russians, having built up the infrastructure, had pulled out, leaving the Mongolians independent but a little helpless. Most people were unemployed and therefore had poor diets. I have never seen so many children stumbling about with bowed legs, the result of rickets. In the shops there was only beetroot and nothing else, which is why the missionaries were glad of the food I had brought them from China.

In the city there was only one restaurant, and the missionaries had an idea for each of us to take half a dozen of the hungry people hanging around and buy them a meal as our guests. We did this, but the amount that was served barely filled the middle of a saucer – a few teaspoons full of vegetables and a minute piece of "meat". However, it was better than nothing. It was a great way to witness to the love of God and we were blessed that some of the Mongolians even spoke a little English. We prayed for God to intervene and help them.

I wondered if there were any Jewish people in the city, but on enquiring I was told they had all left with the Russians. Surely, I thought, there might be one or two left? Further enquiry resulted in being directed to a lady who worked in the library. She spoke very good English and invited me to her flat. As we talked, it transpired she was indeed Jewish. Praise the Lord!

She spoke of her situation. Her Buddhist Mongolian husband had died and now she had the possibility to go to Israel, so I was able to tell her how to go about it. She also told me of a Jewish man she knew and gave me his contact details. Other than him, she didn't know of any other Jewish people in Ulan Bator.

I went to see the man, explaining my reason for visiting. He was a businessman, married to a very beautiful Mongolian lady, and they had three charming children. He had no interest in making aliyah (immigrating to Israel) but thought a visit might be a good idea. However, I knew that once visited, Israel has her own way of getting into people's hearts and drawing them back. I was sure that God had His finger on this family and eventually they would find their way to the Promised Land.

~

Thinking about my flight to Moscow, I went to the travel agent's office as I had been advised in China. Still there were no seats available. I still believed that the Lord had given me the date I was to travel so arranged with the clerk to return the next day to see if there had been any cancellations. She assured me there wouldn't be and pressured me to buy a ticket for the next week. I wouldn't do this, however, knowing that when God gives you a time for something, it is important to stick to it.

I arrived the next day and to my amazement was greeted with the question, "How are you going to pay for your flight?" There was no acknowledgement that there had been a cancellation. There just seemed to be a seat available. They only took American Express travellers' cheques which again was incredible as that was all I had! God knows everything in advance and I had felt led to buy these particular cheques weeks before, and what is more, I had the exact amount, no change. What an amazing God we have!

Kiev

My flight took me to Moscow and from there I took the train to Kiev. I stayed in Kiev for a month with a pastor and his wife from the former "underground" church.

Together we did some hospital visiting in the evenings. There were wounded soldiers from the war in Afghanistan and children terminally ill from the effects of the Chernobyl disaster. We gave the children books that told the gospel in pictures, as they couldn't read. Of the 145 soldiers, all but four committed their lives to Jesus!

During the day I spent some time assisting in the offices of a Christian ministry called "Exobus" which ran buses taking Jewish people from distant towns to the airport in Kiev, on their way to a new life in Israel. It was a wonderful work. The distances between towns in Ukraine can be huge, and twice we did the eight-hour journey from Kiev to Dnepropetrovsk and back, bringing about 40 people each time to the airport. It was a two-day trip with an overnight stop. My job was to assist people with boarding the bus, providing drinks needed en route and helping the olim (intending immigrants to Israel) to fill out customs cards. Normally I am travel-sick on buses, especially those that are joggled about on the poor Ukrainian roads, but I was perfectly fine, not nauseous at all! This was all valuable experience which God used when I later worked with Gustav Scheller in Ebenezer. The Lord wastes nothing.

As the weeks rolled by I began to get tired and felt it was time to go back to the UK. I had been travelling and living out of my suitcase for some time. But how was I to get back? I knew that God wanted me to return by bus, but He had not directed me to book anything. One day in the Exobus office I overheard people talking about one of the buses needing to go back to the UK for maintenance and discussing which staff members might go back with it. I felt prompted to ask about it and they said that I could go with it if I wished. God had provided again, hallelujah. The journey took five days. I was exhausted!

~

Back in the UK I reflected on what the Lord had done. Everything He had shown me to do had been achieved. In addition, marvellous tales came out later which were very encouraging. It didn't seem that much had been achieved in Tibet, but I found out that when there had been floods in certain parts of China, the government had moved hundreds of families to Lhasa to live in the high-rise flats there. Some of these were Christians and they started up a small church. This had grown and the gospel was being taken into the surrounding villages. Tibetans were receiving salvation through Jesus Christ!

Like Hannah and me, many people had made such prayer journeys into Tibet. The Lord had heard and knew when the heavenly censer was full of the prayers of His saints. It was all His doing and the glory was His alone.

In Mongolia too there are fellowships of believers springing up, aided by the missionaries there. God is building His Church. He alone leads people to make journeys to pray in certain places and to speak to particular people. He has the plan and as His saints obey He brings forth the eternal fruit, whether it is encouragement, salvation or the return of His Jewish people to their Promised Land.

It took me three full weeks to recover from the travelling but I was content in what had been achieved. In the meantime Gustav was in the process of organizing a ship to take Jews from Odessa on the Black Sea to Haifa in Israel. I had felt sometime before that God wanted me to assist with this. Was this the next thing I was to do?

3

God Always Has a Plan –
Kamchatka

*Bring My sons from afar and My daughters from the ends of
the earth ...*

(Isaiah 43:6b)

It was 1987 and the Communist system in the Soviet Union was
beginning to crumble. Even so, the KGB was still active and
Christians continued to be persecuted. There were of course state-
registered churches, which were open to give pretence of religious
freedom, but those attending were watched closely. Personal Bibles
were of course forbidden and, for outsiders, smuggling them into
the country was a risky business. Thankfully, by the grace of God I
managed to bring some in for a small church. There were many such
"underground" churches, but whenever the authorities discovered
them, the believers paid a heavy price for worshipping in secret.

"She wants you to get some Bibles for her," someone explained, as
a stocky, ruddy-cheeked lady gave me a slip of paper with a message
in Russian on it. I agreed to do so, not realizing the problems that
would be involved. At this time I was living in Israel and when I got
back I showed the Russian message to someone who could translate
it all. It included the lady's name, Galina, and her address in a place
called Korf. It took me a little time to find it on a map and when I did

I was surprised to discover it was in the far north-east corner of the Kamchatka Peninsula. *How will I get there*? I wondered.

~

The Soviet Far East was used for Stalin's Gulag – the system of prisons and slave-labour camps where men, women and children who had committed some misdemeanour were sent from all over the Soviet Union. They were put to work on various building projects and literally worked to death, their bodies being thrown into the foundations of roads that stretched across the region. Some of these individuals may have committed crimes but often had done nothing. They were simply picked up by the authorities and usually at night so as not to cause alarm in the neighbourhood. They were transported to the Gulag and put to work as slaves on whatever was the latest project in that area. Most of the towns, cities, roads, railways and airports were constructed by these slave workers. The centre for distribution of prisoners was Magadan, a town on the coast, and this name seemed still to instil fear in the populace.

Among the present-day population are the children and grandchildren of those who were sent into exile, some of them Jews. Others have settled in the region voluntarily because the wages are higher than in other places. Others still are native peoples of the region, cousins of Alaskan Eskimos and tribes from further inland on the border with China. So, strange as it may seem, Jewish people were sometimes found living alongside white Russians and Siberian tribespeople. The Lord said He would scatter His people to the far ends of the earth and this happened as survivors of the Gulag camps settled in the areas surrounding their prisons when the penal system collapsed; after all, it was often too difficult for them to go back to their original areas due to the isolation of the camps.

~

Several years passed and in 1985 I had returned to the UK from Armenia where I had handed over the aliyah work to the Truth Church in Yerevan. Each month a small number of Jews returned to Israel by flying to Odessa in Ukraine and joining Ebenezer's ship for the voyage to Haifa.

I was not sure what the Lord had for me next and was using the time for a rest. Meeting up with my friend Hannah, I learned she had been again to Khabarovsk in the Russian Far East, visiting her friend Laura and taking humanitarian aid for the Jewish people and both aid and Christian teaching materials for the new churches there. She just happened to mention that Laura had spent time in Petropavlovsk-Kamchatka. At the mention of the word "Kamchatka" a small "bell" seemed to ring in my head. I related to Hannah how I had met Galina and said that she lived in Korf. We could not be sure she still lived there, but it made sense to ask Laura if she could try to make contact for us. This was agreed and, sensing we should go to Kamchatka, we began to pray, seeking to know God's plan.

The Lord revealed that He wanted us to visit four areas in the far east of Russia: Khabarovsk, Magadan, Petropavlovsk-Kamchatka and Korf. To go to these places we would need visas, but as they were in the Khabarovsk region it transpired we could visit them all by just applying for a visa for Khabarovsk. This made things much more straightforward.

In Korf our contact of course was Galina, but for the other towns we were given names of pastors by various people. Travelling and ministering in the former Soviet Union (fSU) necessitates having contacts so we were grateful for these names. In addition the Lord gave us a "word" from Exodus 23:20: "Behold, I am going to send an angel before you to guard you along the way and to bring you into the place which I have prepared." How true this proved to be. We had no idea then but this trip was going to be one of our most amazing journeys!

Just before we left England, Gustav Scheller (of Operation Exodus) met up with me. He had started the sailings from Odessa to Haifa taking olim (Jewish people making aliyah) to Israel. Since he had previously helped finance two of the planes from Armenia, he wanted to know what the Lord was telling me to do next. When I told him I was going to the far east of the fSU he was excited – he was going there too – and only a week or two after me. In God's plans there are no coincidences, only "God-incidences", as we were to find out!

~

The route Hannah and I were to take took us from England to Anchorage, Alaska, and from there direct to Khabarovsk. The plan was to use this city as a base, leaving most of our luggage, and from there travel to the other places. For each city we purchased a large suitcase and filled them with Bibles, books (many by Derek Prince) and other Christian teaching materials. In addition we included warm clothing and other gifts plus our own personal things. All were over the weight limit for the airlines but when we explained that most of the weight was humanitarian aid we were thankfully not charged. This was a real answer to prayer!

Arriving safely in Khabarovsk, we left two of the suitcases there with Hannah's friend and flew by Aeroflot airlines to Petropavlovsk in Kamchatka. For just these two cases we were charged $140 excess!

We were to be met at the airport by both my contact, Galina, and someone from the local church whom we did not know. Both would be expecting to look after us. This was a bit of a concern, as we did not want to cause confusion or upset anyone. I remember praying that the Lord would sort it out and of course He did. At the airport were a group of people waiting for us; there was the pastor, Anatoly, a young lad of 16 called Ura (our interpreter), a lady called Natalia and, to our surprise, Galina. We asked how she knew the others and it transpired that Natalia had seen Galina and had felt led to ask whom she was meeting. They soon found out they were waiting for the same two ladies from England and so Natalia had invited

Galina to join her group. Everyone was happy and of course I needn't have worried. What an amazing Heavenly Father we have! We were whisked away for a wonderful meal that had been specially prepared for us and then shown to our accommodation – a flat belonging to two girls who had left for Bible school in Moscow.

The next day we tried to purchase our airline tickets for the relatively short flight to Korf but found there was a problem: our visas did not allow us to visit Korf. We thought Korf was included but found that the problem was the military status of the area. Much of it was closed to foreign visitors, as it was a home to atomic submarines and army camps. Because of the many earthquakes and volcanoes there were no roads between the towns and no railways.

Galina was to accompany us back to Korf and had spent all her savings on the trip to meet us in Petropavlovsk. How were we going to tell her that we could not go? Once again the Lord had everything in hand. Natalia, the lady who had invited Galina to join her group at the airport, had heard of our dilemma. She came to us and said, "Give me your passports." It transpired that in Communist days she had been "someone" and still had contacts. She took us from office to office, speaking to various officials. Amazingly we were soon buying our tickets to Korf ! All the problems had been sorted out with the bureaucracy, and the next day we were off to Korf with a radiant Galina! It turned out she was an amazing sister. She had an unbelieving husband and was the only Christian in Korf. She had been praying for 12 years that the Lord would do something in her town. We had arrived! What a lesson in faith and persistence!

The aeroplane was tiny. Boarding was through an opening in the underside of the fuselage. You had to carry your luggage through this opening and put it on a shelf and then find a seat. Some of the seats, we discovered, had broken backs that would not stay up so we learned on subsequent flights that one had to be quick to get a safe seat. The seat belts had to be tied with a knot, and on take-off the engines made a terrific noise. We wondered just how reliable these planes were!

Korf

A little over an hour later we arrived in Korf. Galina spoke no English so we had to make do with my halting Russian plus a dictionary. I attempted to explain to her that our cases were heavy and that we would need transport. "Taxi?" I asked.

"No, no," she said, and indicated that we should walk.

The plane had landed on a tiny airstrip in front of some wooden buildings we had seen from the air and mistakenly taken to be sheds. Leaving the plane we pulled our cases into the arrivals area. An official looked at our documents and demanded to know the purpose of our visit, saying, "You are not allowed here." There was a little discussion in Russian among the officials, but since the return flight was a week away there was little they could do and in the end they let us through. Hallelujah! When God wants something to happen He makes sure it does. Natalia had definitely been sent to help us.

Once outside we realized why Galina had said there would be no taxis – there were no connecting roads, only earth tracks! Korf was just a little settlement on the coast where transport was by helicopter or small plane. There wasn't even a railway.

The cold had started to creep into our clothes and we were glad of our thermal underwear and warm anoraks. The wooden buildings along the airstrip that we had thought were sheds were actually houses and Galina lived in one. She found a man to carry our cases along the earthen path to her door. Just inside was a welcoming wood-burning stove in the corner of a small hallway. We were soon inside enjoying a hot cup of Russian tea. We unpacked our cases and presented Galina with the Bibles, teaching materials and gifts of warm clothes and gloves. She was overwhelmed and beamed with joy. In fact all the while we were in Korf she never seemed to stop glowing with happiness!

Nearby there were a number of two-storey faded blue wooden houses built in a square. The ladies from these houses were friends with Galina and had started showing an interest in her faith. They were the beginning of a tiny new church and needed Bibles. The children too were drawn to Galina's house, attracted by her love. They started to read the children's books we had brought and began to ask questions about Jesus.

The children told us about their short summer which they were eagerly awaiting. They would go out into the tundra areas looking for berries and mushrooms. These were preserved for use in the long winter. They laughingly pointed to the ceiling, showing how high the snow gets, and told us that motor sledges and skis were the mode of transport in the winter.

It was hard for us as Westerners to imagine how they existed in such conditions. Galina took us outside and showed us her plastic-covered greenhouse where she grew potatoes, tomatoes, cucumbers and peppers, which she preserved. When possible, salmon and other fish were caught locally, and the men hunted various animals in their seasons. It was a subsistence existence. To see Westerners visit them was for these people quite a novelty.

After absorbing the impact of these physical and cultural factors our thoughts turned to Jewish people. Could there be any here at the ends of the earth? Isaiah prophesied, "Bring My sons from afar and My daughters from the ends of the earth" (Isaiah 43:6b), so there should be some. Galina confirmed for us that there were indeed Jewish people living locally and took us to meet them. There were four families and we talked with them about God's call to them to go to Israel, the Promised Land of their forefathers. We explained how the aliyah programme works and how the Israeli government gives assistance in finding jobs and somewhere to live.

Despite painting an encouraging picture of life in Israel and telling them how anti-Semitism was growing throughout the world, they showed no interest. They felt safe in Korf. They were far from anywhere and said that no one knew they were Jewish. This revealed that they were living in denial as we had found them precisely because their neighbours knew they were Jewish. Only one man, his wife and son were interested. I say "wife" but they were never officially married though they had been together for 18 years. This form of relationship was common in that area because to formalize the arrangement meant travelling to Petropavlovsk, a journey that was too expensive for some couples. For the couple to make aliyah they would need to be officially married, for the man's wife was not Jewish; but if they formalized their marriage now, the Israeli consul might suspect it was a marriage of convenience. In the end a sad turn of events sorted the problem out, for the "wife" was terminally ill and a year later passed away. Eventually the man and his son made aliyah by themselves and we heard they were very happy.

Many years later we heard that an earthquake had hit Korf, destroying all the little houses that we had visited near the airport. Thankfully Galina and her husband were rescued, as were others, and taken by helicopter to Petropavlovsk. From there they were sent back to Kiev. We do not know about the Jewish people we had visited. We hope they escaped and had made aliyah. It served as a reminder that there are times and seasons for doing things and of the importance of heeding God's call when it comes.

Tilichiki

Korf was a tiny settlement of about 200 people and we soon had explored it all. We were there for a week and Galina suggested that we visited a children's home in another small settlement called Tilichiki. It was a home for "native" children, that is, those of the tribes that had inhabited the region before the Russians had come. The children were sick with TB and Galina thought we could perhaps take them some of the clothes we had brought.

Under the old Soviet system, children from rural areas were put in boarding schools in the towns and only went home in the holidays. We visited the school and found the children playing outside in the cold. They were shy and noticeably different from Russian children, with their slanted eyes, olive skin and other Mongolian-type features.

When we asked where their homes were, we were told, "Up there", with fingers pointing northwards.

The headmistress welcomed us inside and proceeded to tell us about the school. Most of the pupils had returned home for the summer, but those that were present had remained because they had TB, which was common in the area. The headmistress implied that the poor things were subnormal, tapping her head with her finger to give emphasis. However, when I looked at the children's colourful paintings showing clear images of reindeer and of their people hunting and fishing, both Hannah and I agreed they were far from subnormal. Perhaps the headmistress had meant "primitive". We asked her where the children had come from and, as previously, we were told, "Up north". We wondered what there was in this region to the north and when we consulted a map we discovered it was a place called Chukotka. We both felt we should go there soon.

~

The next week we found it hard to say goodbye to our friends in Korf but our time had come to an end and we had to go back to Petropavlovsk. Here we met the wonderful Christians again who had greeted us on our arrival. The pastor, Anatoly, was overwhelmed by the books we gave him. He pastored five churches, two of which were inside prisons. We met the Jewish Agency representative and leaders of the Jewish community who were eager to work with us and with Ebenezer Operation Exodus. They told us of many areas where Jewish scientists worked but which were closed to visitors, places where military developments such as nuclear bombs were taking place! In this situation the Lord again had His ways of getting in and once more used Natalia to go in and find these people.

Returning to Khabarovsk we found our flight was scheduled a day early, but it turned out to be the Hand of God as there was an earthquake in Petropavlovsk on the day we should have travelled, causing the airport to close for ten days. All of our ongoing flights would have been cancelled and the rest of our trip impossible. What an amazing God we serve! He knows every detail of every day!

4

More Far East Adventures

Thus says the Lord God,
"Behold, I will lift up My hand to the nations
And set up My standard to the peoples;
And they will bring your sons in their bosom,
And your daughters will be carried on their shoulders."

(Isaiah 49:22)

Magadan

After saying "Farewell" to our new friends in Petropavlovsk we flew with Aeroflot airlines to Magadan where we were met by a man named Boris who had been sent by the pastor. Our flight had been delayed and he had waited four hours for us but dismissed this as "normal"! The airport was 50 kilometres from the town and Boris informed us that our route took us along what was infamously known as "Death Road". The explanation regarding its name was harrowing. In Stalin's time the road surface was rough, and as the area was part of the Gulag (prison system) prisoners were each allotted a part of the road to maintain and keep in good order. Often they had no tools or materials and had to use their hands or whatever they could find to work with. The harsh weather conditions in this part of Siberia made this nigh impossible, but nevertheless the penalty for failing in this duty was dire. If the prison governor's car gave him a rough ride on a particular stretch of road, the prisoner responsible was made to dig a hole in the offending place. He was then shot and his body buried in the hole and another prisoner took over his job. Countless bodies lay beneath "Death Road" – no one knew how many. It was a graphic example of the cruelty of Stalin's Gulag system.

It was impossible to escape the prison-like atmosphere in Magadan – oppression seemed to pervade every street corner, every building, and struggling against this was the landscape. It could be beautiful in parts, particularly the beach which was a little like north Cornwall.

In the Gulag period, prisoners were brought by ship from Vladivostok after a horrendous journey on the Trans-Siberian Railway, standing up for eight days with little food or water; many did not survive. The Gulag authorities did not care of course. Prisoners were worked until they died anyway. Those that were among the first to arrive and survived the journeys by train and ship had nowhere to live and had to build their own temporary shelters. When these were finished they lived in them while building more substantial ones for themselves and those prisoners who would follow. Winter temperatures often reached minus 50 degrees Celsius and the transport ships could only dock at a point far out on the sea ice. The prisoners had to make their way across this to the land and, being ill-clad and on a poor diet, thousands perished.

When the Gulag system was eventually terminated any survivors had no choice but to settle in the area and try to eke out a living; this was evidenced by hundreds of little shacks and rusty vehicles which sat in clusters on the rubbish-strewn seashore.

Further inland was the town, built by slave labour in the 1950s; it was full of drab, dingy high-rise apartment blocks. Nothing in it was attractive. In glorious contrast, God's creation of beautiful forest-clad hills, some still snow-capped, drew one's eye to more pleasant sights.

~

Our driver, Boris, took us to stay with a family where the father was Jewish. He told us that the pastor was also Jewish and that they all wanted to go to make aliyah. In their eagerness they had set up a meeting for us the next morning. There we met the believers. This little church was new, a spark of light and a banner of victory that had emerged despite the Soviet era when Communists were determined to destroy Christianity. Many Christians had been brought here to die; Jews too, just for believing in God, wanting to keep their faith and learning Hebrew with the ultimate desire to go to Israel.

Here, as in Kamchatka, we found wonderful, lively, enthusiastic believers, full of joy and "on fire" for God. New churches had been established, like beautiful plants thriving in a desert, germinating in "soil" soaked in the blood of the martyrs who had gone before. The one we were going to this morning met in an old cinema. We gazed at the people's bright faces; they were eager to hear why we had come. After a glorious time of worship, we talked to them, through an interpreter, about the ingathering of the Jewish people and about how Gentiles are called by God to assist them. We read Scriptures such as Isaiah 49:22:

> *Behold, I will lift up My hand in an oath to the nations,*
> *And set up My standard for the peoples;*
> *They shall bring your sons in their arms,*
> *And your daughters shall be carried on their shoulders.*

> (nkjv)

They got very excited as they saw the prophecies for themselves!

As I looked at them thumbing through the pages of the Scriptures, I marvelled at how each of them had a Bible and remembered the days not so long ago when Bibles were forbidden by the authorities and how I had been involved in smuggling some in. Now they each had one!

They were keen to start contacting the Jews and telling them about the opportunity to make aliyah so they arranged a meeting for the local Jewish community to come the next morning! When the time came many Jews arrived, some of them Messianic, some of them not, but all together, as if it was normal and without any one of them finding it a problem. (This was no doubt helped by the fact that they were meeting, not in a church building, but an old cinema.) We read the Scriptures to them from Isaiah, Jeremiah and Ezekiel where the prophets foretold of God's call to return to the land of their forefathers, and they received it with great joy. We told them what Israel does for olim (new immigrants) to help them settle in, learn Hebrew and find accommodation and jobs. We told them about the work of Ebenezer and the volunteers that would come and assist them and show them how to apply to go to Israel. They asked many questions and the meeting was soon buzzing with talk among themselves about "going home"!

One lady, though, came to us in tears. She had a sad story. It seemed that her grown-up daughter had made aliyah with her husband and little girl some time ago but the marriage had failed and they had divorced. She had then met and married an Arab, but he didn't want the little girl and so she had been sent back to Russia to live with her grandmother. The daughter had intended to return for the girl at some point but this had never happened and matters had been complicated because she had given birth to another child and this marriage too was in trouble. The grandmother had lost contact with her daughter and had heard nothing for some time. She was very distressed and gave me the last address she had of her daughter (the Hebrew written phonetically in Russian script which I could not understand!), begging me to try and help her. I promised to do my best but knew it would not be easy.

Komsomolske and Amursk

After a few days in Magadan we returned to Khabarovsk. Here it was hot and sticky and the air was filled with midges and mosquitoes.

These pests got into your eyes, nose and mouth with alacrity and there was no way to stop them.

We found out that Gustav and Elsa Scheller had arrived and, talking with them, we made the decision to go to different areas. They headed for Birobidjan, a region Stalin had set apart for the settlement of Jews, and where they could meet Jewish leaders, while Hannah and I headed for a town called Komsomolske-na-Amure. We were going there to meet two Jewish families who we knew wanted to make aliyah. A local church member made contact with some believers there to help us, and a local friend, Igor, offered to drive us there in his "new" second-hand Japanese minibus.

The journey was an adventure in itself – 250 kilometres, on a road of rocks, stones and potholes and through a forest. It was a seven-and-a-half-hour trip with no shops or Little Chefs – in fact no stops at all. We reached Komsomolske hot, sticky and very thirsty. The pastor and his wife thankfully were waiting for us and informed us that the two families we had come to visit had actually gone to Israel two months earlier! The journey, however, was not wasted as we could see many Jewish people walking in the streets, and the new local church was very anxious to help them in their preparations to make aliyah.

One of the Christian families prepared a meal for us, which was kind as they had so little themselves, and after we had finished encouraged us to go on to the next town, Amursk, because a meeting had been set up for us there. The son of the family drove us and within an hour and a half we had arrived. It turned out not to be a Jewish meeting but another lively new church. They wanted to hear what we had to say to them but could not provide an interpreter and as we had not brought one ourselves we had a potential problem. However, I felt the Holy Spirit urging me to try out my Russian so I did and was able, totally under His anointing, to share for about half an hour why Christians should help Jews – and they understood it too. They were thrilled with what I shared and the pastor encouraged them further, and together they prayed about being involved with Ebenezer and the work of helping the aliyah. Praise God!

It turned out that 12 Jewish families had been invited to the meeting but had been too afraid to come. After the meeting we were taken to visit one Jewish home where they explained the position in which Jews in that region found themselves. Many of those who had survived the Gulag period had no documents, having destroyed them long ago to hide their Jewish identity, and it seemed to them that the possibility of applying to the Israeli consul was unrealistic and their situation hopeless. In response we suggested that they check the archives that were in every town as there might be copies of their documents there. We also showed them the Scriptures that demonstrated God's call to make aliyah and told them that this was why God had sent us to them and explained that He would make a way. They were much encouraged and promised to tell their friends. They wanted to go to Israel as soon as possible.

We stayed overnight and set off the next morning, not relishing the long journey. Igor drove at a good speed over the stony road. It was full of potholes, many of them quite deep. It was while trying to avoid one of these that the vehicle went into a terrible skid, out of control, lurching violently from one side of the road to the other in ever widening arcs, getting faster and faster, threatening to plunge off the road and down the embankment. At any second it could turn on its side. It was very frightening. A fast-approaching lorry added to the danger. We shouted "Jesus, Jesus, help us!" and it suddenly slowed right down just before the lorry reached us, something that was really impossible! We stared at each other in wonder! Once again the Lord had saved my life and the others too. We shouted our praises to God in relief and I remembered the last time something like this had happened on a journey to Nagorno Karabakh (see my other book, *The Ingathering of Israel*).

~

On arrival back in Khabarovsk we met with Gustav and Elsa to compare "notes". They too had had a profitable journey and returned with good news of another church that wanted to be part of the work. The result of these two trips was that Ebenezer were able to open an office in Khabarovsk and many Jewish people were assisted in making aliyah from the region.

We returned to England jet-lagged. Our bodies did not know which time zone we were in and it took us a while to get used to British Summer Time, so we were ready for a good rest. Praise God, it had been a worthwhile trip.

Beer-Sheva, Israel

Three months later I was in Israel and hoped to find the daughter of the lady in Magadan who had been so distressed and asked me for my help. We serve a wonderful, compassionate Heavenly Father who knows all things, who loves us in ways beyond our understanding – and He understood the need of this family. The address I had been given was Hebrew but written in Russian Cyrillic script. All I understood was that it was somewhere in Beer-Sheva. I was in Jerusalem and it was Friday morning. Transport in Israel shuts down about 4.00 p.m. ready for *Shabbat* (the Sabbath). This meant that because it was a journey of about one to two hours each way I would need to leave Beer-Sheva by 2.00 p.m. to allow for the return journey. I protested a little to the Lord but felt Him impress upon me that it was indeed the time to go and find this address and that He would watch over me.

I caught the bus in Jerusalem about 9.00 a.m. and duly arrived in the Central Bus Station in Beer-Sheva around 11.00 a.m. I had no idea where I needed to go to find the address and was not even sure that the daughter, Anna, still lived there. But even if that were the case, I reasoned, perhaps someone would know where she lived. Suddenly into my head came the thought, *Take a taxi.* I had been sent on too many trips by the Lord to ignore thoughts like this so, committing this to Him, I prayed for the right driver, someone helpful, to come along.

Outside the bus station a taxi-driver saw me and came over. I showed him the address and he understood it immediately. He invited me into his cab and we were off. He drove for what seemed like quite a long way and I began to wonder if he was cheating me. But no, we arrived at a run-down area of poor-quality blocks of flats, raised up on pillars, three storeys high. All around was sand. There were no trees, flowers or footpaths – just sand where Ethiopian children were playing. It was very hot.

The driver pointed to the flats vaguely and indicated that the address was there somewhere. He had used the meter and did not overcharge me, so after giving him a tip I left him and made my way to the flats, wondering how I was going to get back – there were no other taxis about. The Lord had impressed upon me that He would look after me so I had to trust Him.

I had been in this situation before and had found God faithfully directing me, so I looked at the apartment blocks in front of me and asked the Lord, "Which one?" Within me I had a feeling of assurance that it was the middle block so I went over and looked at the front of the postal boxes, but there were no names on them. "Which floor, Lord?" I asked and once more somehow knew it was the third. Up the narrow stairs I went. Two doors faced each other on the small landing. "Which one?" I felt urged to go to the left one and rang the bell. No reply. I tried again. Maybe it hadn't worked, so I rapped on the door with my knuckles – still no response.

On the other door was a Russian name. After knocking there, a young man answered and in Russian assured me that a lady called Anna did indeed live in the other flat. More determined than ever I rang again, knocked and called out loudly, "Anna, Anna!" The door opened just a little and a pair of eyes peeped through the gap. In mixed Russian and Hebrew we had a short conversation before a young lady allowed me to come in. Success at last – it was indeed Anna! I had found her and only because the Lord had led me. Hallelujah!

She was obviously curious about why a foreigner was visiting her. She knew no English so we had to continue in a mixture of Russian and Hebrew. I told her about visiting Magadan and how I had met her mother who was worried and desperate to make contact with her and that she had asked me to help find her. She was very defensive at first and then began to cry, very upset at the situation in which she found herself. She poured out her troubles, telling me that the man she had married had proved to be a wealthy Bedouin who already had a wife and family. Having married Anna, he duly provided for her and their child but lived elsewhere and only visited her. She was angry about being wife number two, about living alone, looking after their baby all by herself and having no friends and no real life of her own. The area was drab too. There were few shops, no park nearby and nothing to do. She allowed me to comfort her and sobbed in my arms. I asked her what she would like to do. She said she thought life would be better in Tel Aviv where she could get a job but couldn't see how this was possible as even there she would be alone looking after her little girl. The situation seemed bleak but eventually our mixture of languages caused her to smile and she made me a cup of tea.

Soon Anna's little girl woke up, a pretty child of about two years old. She wore a gold necklace and earrings, a gift from her father. I asked if I could take a picture of them both, but Anna would only allow one of her little girl, none of herself. It took some while before I managed to persuade her to write a letter to her mother for me to deliver. She very much wanted to go and see her other daughter in Russia, but again felt the situation was hopeless as her passport needed renewing and she had no money for airfares. I talked to her about her Heavenly Father and said that I believed if we prayed together about the situation He would meet her need. She doubted this but nevertheless allowed me to pray for her and finish in the Name of Yeshua (Jesus).

Needing to get back to town for the last bus to Jerusalem, I indicated to Anna that I needed to leave. She was now reluctant to be parted from me but ordered a taxi, and soon, after an emotional hug and farewell, I left her and made my way back to Jerusalem.

~

About four months later I was back in Magadan and tried to find Anna's mother. I expected that she would show up at the meeting we invited everyone to but she didn't, and upon asking one or two of those present I was told that she had moved. No one knew to where.

After trying different places I explained the situation to the Jewish family I was staying with. "I'll find her," said my hostess. "Give me the paper with her name."

That evening she returned with a printed sheet containing the virtual life-story of Anna's mother, where she was born, where she was educated, the various places she had lived, her marriage details – in fact a complete breakdown of her life. Plus, and most importantly, her present address! I was amazed but I discovered every citizen had a record like this in the archive office!

We took a taxi to find the address, which proved to be the basement of a run-down block of flats. We rang the bell and a few minutes later who should answer? Not Anna's mother but Anna herself all the way from Israel! We fell into each other's arms. She explained that her Arab husband had agreed to pay for her and the child to visit her mother and Anna had decided, once in Russia, not to go back to him. She would stay and teach Hebrew to would- be immigrants, encouraging them to make aliyah. She would then save up some money for a fresh start in Israel herself. Her mother and older daughter were planning to go with her and settle in Tel Aviv. She was a very different Anna now, so bright and full of hopes and plans, chatting happily again in Hebrew and Russian. What a wonderful God we serve! He had arranged all this and rescued this Jewish family from their unhappy situation. It was a wonderful ending to a sad story and a great answer to our prayers!

5

To the Ends of the Earth

I will go before you and make the rough places smooth;
I will shatter the doors of bronze and cut through their iron bars.
I will give you the treasures of darkness
And hidden wealth of secret places, So that you may know that
it is I, the Lord, the God of Israel, who calls you by your name.
(Isaiah 45:2–3)

Once back from our adventures in the Russian Far East, we set about
checking just what place was "north" of the Kamchatka Peninsula.
It proved to be a region called Chukotka. We later discovered that it
is also known as "Krai Zimlay", which in Russian means End of the
Earth. Very aptly named, as we found.

Hannah and I both knew the Lord wanted us to go there, so
began to pray into this. It seemed to us that the best plan was to go
via Alaska, but first we would need to check out the route and obtain
visas. We applied for the latter at the London Russian Embassy.
Our friend in Anchorage who had helped us on our previous trip
to the Russian Far East was all set to help us again and planned the
route across the Bering Sea while constantly assuring us that our
visas would soon be provided. With this confidence we booked our

flights, allowing three weeks for going into Chukotka and expecting to set up everything from Anchorage.

Time passed and a day or two before we were due to depart, the Russian Embassy informed us that we could not have visas to go to Chukotka. No reason was given, just a point-blank refusal. When we protested over the telephone, they abruptly hung up. We tried again and received the same refusal, so we asked to go to Magadan instead, thinking we could travel north from there.

"No, not for Magadan either," was the reply. "Why not?" we asked.

"Ha – we know what you are doing," they said. "You can only have a visa for Moscow."

We felt flat. What should we do? What was the problem? At this point, we had no idea. The Lord had led us to believe we should go there, so surely He would make the way?

We prayed and consulted friends, who all agreed that we should go to Alaska as planned and see if we could get visas from there. Also, we could find out more. We set off to Anchorage where our friend had linked up with a pastor called Joe. He proved to be a great blessing. The Lord had sent him into Chukotka years before, when Communism came to an end, to preach the gospel. He had gone across to the first town, called Providenya. There was no church there but he had met a lady who taught English, a Communist willing to translate for him.

Inevitably she heard the gospel and became a very committed believer who now pastors the church Joe planted.

Joe gave us a lot of useful information. First of all, Chukotka was now a closed military zone, being so close to the USA. Permission to enter the area was needed from the governor, police, the military and it seemed just about everyone. Missionaries were not allowed. Joe had recently had to return to Alaska after living in Providenya for several years with his wife and children. The latest governor had made strict rules regarding missionaries, and tourists were not allowed in either.

Only exchange groups of entomologists, seismologists, hunters and fishermen could be arranged. Did we count as "fishers"? Not really, certainly not in the accepted sense! A company called Bering Air ran charter flights for such groups and it was possible to book spare seats but the planes were small, six- or nine-seater models with little room for luggage. They usually flew at midday in the short summer season if the cloud cleared for long enough, the journey taking about an hour.

Joe also told us there were now small churches in other towns; the capital being Anadyr. All journeys had to be by plane or helicopter as there were no connecting roads or railways between towns. Any flights had to be booked locally and were few and far between, maybe one flight a week only. If we ever did get there it sounded like we'd need a month! Added to this, there was no Russian embassy or even a consulate in Alaska, the nearest being just a consulate office in Seattle, way south in Washington State. The term "Mission Impossible" sprang to mind. Joe was going back to Providenya and offered to help us if we did get there. His wife and three children would be there too.

We knew that our God was the God of the impossible. He opens doors no one can shut and shuts doors no one can open. We were sure He wanted us to go to Chukotka and so we trusted Him to make a way. He did – and this is how. He is an amazing God!

~

We returned to England to pray and find out how God would bring this trip about. Usually He does things in ways we could not have imagined and this was no exception. A friend, Stephen, had been in Armenia, helping people to find ways to earn a living as there was much unemployment. One day he called us from London to say he had become engaged and asked us if we would come to meet his fiancée, Karen, a beautiful young American lady. Hannah could not go, but I did. Karen asked me many questions while we drank coffee and was very curious about what we did and why. Obviously Stephen had told her a little of our adventures!

"But what are you doing next?" she asked. This proved to be a key question and I told her about our call to Chukotka and explained where it was – opposite Alaska. She was very thoughtful for a while and then said, "I have a friend in Alaska. I think she works for Bering Air and helps people get flights over to Russia. She might even know how to get visas! She is a Christian too. I'll get in touch with her and see what I can find out."

A flood of warmth surged through me and I knew we were on to something. Not long afterwards, we heard from Karen that her friend did indeed set up charter flights and also knew how to apply for visas. (It would actually be an invitation. This would enable us to obtain visas from the Russian Embassy.) Karen said that recently an American woman had married a Russian surgeon from Chukotka and had gone to live there in Providenya – the little town directly across from Alaska. She had asked, and been allowed, to invite small groups from Alaska for cultural exchange trips, whereby she took them to see Eskimos who lived locally along the coastline. Some small groups of six to eight people had been allowed to participate in this venture. Maybe, just maybe, we could be included and so get an invitation. Karen gave us her contact details.

It transpired that this new contact, Janine, lived and worked in Nome, a small city on the far western edge of Alaska. This meant problems with time zones as the area is about halfway round the world from the UK and therefore 11–12 hours behind us. We therefore had to call in the evenings to speak to Janine. When we got through to her she explained the procedure ahead. She would send us the application forms by fax and she would send them to the authorities, together with those of other people applying for fishing or hunting expeditions or for the "culture" trips we had heard of. In fact she said we should put down "cultural exchange" as our own reason for travel.

We studied some maps of Chukotka and put down five towns to visit. This was much more than the "culture trips" in Providenya, but we would need these destinations if we were to travel about. The answer could take about five to six weeks to come back to us. First, the permission had to be personally authorized by the governor of Chukotka, and then by the military and also various other officials. We needed to send $200 each for the governor even to look at our applications. Since the area was designated as "illegal to foreigners", we knew it would truly take a miracle for British people to be allowed to go there.

We planned a three-week prayer attack, fasting one day in three to time in with our applications, and invited our prayer partners to join us as they felt able. Janine told us she had sent off the forms. During one of our prayer times, the Holy Spirit gave me a picture of the governor just flicking up the bottom right-hand corner of each form and signing it without reading it first. Hannah had a picture of the Lord standing behind him with one hand raised as if authorizing the signature! We felt confident we would receive the necessary permission.

A week or two later we heard from Janine that our forms had been signed! And soon we received the necessary invitations to apply for visas. Wow! The Lord had done it. Hallelujah! We felt very sure we should not go to the Russian Embassy in London. Instead we should try at the Russian Consulate in Seattle. We could fly there, stay a few days while the visas were arranged, and then go on from Seattle to Anchorage using Alaskan Airlines. The only problem might be that the Russians in the consulate might contact London…

We set off with cases full of warm clothes plus gifts for the churches and the Jewish people we hoped to find. The Russians in the consulate in Seattle were very friendly. They did not ask why we had not applied in London, but just took the papers and asked for

$100 each to prepare the visas within three days. As one of them looked at the forms, he said in Russian, "Very interesting route!" And in three days, we went back to collect them. What did we have?

Visas for tourists! No tourists were allowed in Chukotka but now we had permission as the visas were in our hands! It was with great excitement we set off to Alaska.

We contacted Janine who promised to find us seats on a charter flight, which she did, so we were soon in Nome awaiting her call. The plane was tiny with just room for our bags somewhere under the wings. The other passengers were all fishermen – big burly fellows – but then we too were going "fishing" so we were in good company!

Providenya

The plane took off from Nome into a clear sky at about midday, and in about an hour we saw land. Suddenly we turned a sharp right, entering a narrow channel to come down swiftly over the sea to land on a strip, which began literally as the sea ended. It was quite awesome.

The customs officials were very curious about us since our visas clearly said "tourists". Also, because we had been told not to look like missionaries we had tried to create a more "worldly" appearance! In a way, maybe I overdid it with the help of daughters and granddaughter. I was wearing jeans (the first and only time for me), many necklaces, bracelets, a bomber jacket, with my hair coloured blonde, much make-up and bright nail varnish. In fact I did not look like my passport photo at all. The man took a ruler and slowly moved down the photo, step by step, comparing me with the picture. In the end I just laughed and said "It is me!" whereupon he laughed too and agreed.

We had been told the customs officials would open our bags and check every item, wanting to know why we had anything unusual. Well, we had Bibles and Christian material, things for any Jews we might find; but they were more interested in our dollars! After carefully counting it and registering how much we had, we were allowed through, our bags untouched! Praise God indeed.

The American lady who was married to the Russian surgeon met us and took us by car to what she called her "hotel". It proved to be a couple of rooms in her flat and it transpired we had to find our own food. She changed some dollars for us and directed us to a small shop. There were cigarettes, chewing gum, tins of tomato paste, some hair clips, but little else. No butter, eggs, cheese, milk, meat, vegetables or fruit. We just managed to find a small loaf of bread! Back at the "hotel", our hostess offered us a meal she had made for her other guests who were taking part in her "cultural exchange". We were thankful to sample some rather greasy, tough, stewed meat and potatoes.

~

The next morning we were better able to take note of our surroundings. We set off for a walk and found another tiny shop where we were able to obtain a can of peas and a can of carrots from India. The shop owner punctured the peas with a knife so that we could open the tin. We shared the contents for breakfast with some of our bread. What did these people live on, we wondered. We had brought some oats, dried fruit, powdered milk and tea bags and it was with these we later made ourselves a sort of muesli and drink.

We contacted Joe, who met us and took us to meet his lovely family. They were planning to return to Alaska fairly soon but he was able to introduce us to the pastor of the little church which he had planted, a wonderful woman called Larissa. She proved to be a great help. Joe had said there were Jewish people in the town so we set off to find them with Larissa's help.

We found a man named Josef and his wife and four children who wanted to go to Israel. He had all the necessary documents but no money to go to Moscow or Khabarovsk to see a consul, and no days off work for another one and a half years! He'd have to wait all that time before he could process his application. Josef knew of other Jewish people in the town in mixed marriages and said he would tell them of the possibility of going to Israel.

Larissa told us about the town and how it was built. It was a small port of about 5,000 people, built to supply ships sailing the Arctic route from Murmansk to Vladivostok. During the 1930s Stalin had decreed that the Arctic Sea should be kept open by icebreakers as an alternative to the Trans-Siberian Railway, the usual route to Vladivostok from Moscow. Small towns were built along the route to supply the ships and sadly these were built by slave labour, like so many other towns in the Russian Far East we had heard about.

Each town had a power station fired by coal, which was delivered by barges during the very limited summertime – a month at the most. The coal was dumped on the seashore and used from there. The power station was kept working all year because even in the summer, although it might be light all day, the temperature rarely rose above 5 °C and dropped to below 0 °C at night. This explained the blackened surfaces of the buildings and why our clothes were covered in sooty specks. We probably saw the town at its worst, since for about nine to ten months of the year it is covered in deep snow. Once it begins to thaw, huge puddles uncover broken glass, bricks, and piles of rubble that litter the streets. It seemed nothing ever got cleared up. Black coal-dust mingled with the drifting dirt along the roads, and murky-looking puddles stretched from side to side, with ice lingering at the edges.

The area is mountainous; there are no trees or flowers and little grass to be seen. To build the town, ledges had been cut into the mountainsides so that faceless blocks of flats could be built along them, but leaving a passageway behind them, with steps up to each ledge. Many buildings were empty and falling down, while others were in dire need of repair, giving an air of decay. The port was hardly used any more and the shops had little to offer, leaving the people to struggle on a meagre diet.

Wandering behind the hideous blocks of flats, we noticed some small, shed-like structures that proved to be where those who were enterprising kept chickens and rabbits. Sometimes, with plastic covers, some managed to grow a few vegetables during the short summer weeks. We were astonished. The long, light summer days, when the sun hardly set, could be bright at times, and even feel warm; though for us the sun's impact was slight to say the least.

Occasionally the weather would be broken by heavy showers, low cloud and mist, or with a wind to remind you where you were – right in the Arctic!

~

We could only stay a few days in Providenya so Larissa took us to buy tickets to Anadyr, the capital of the region. The air link of three flights a week seemed to be very busy for no apparent reason. However, we did get tickets for the flight the next day, which for this airline was unusual. Larissa gave us details of a pastor in Anadyr and we promised to stay in touch. Meantime, she said she would contact other Jewish folk she knew about – each married to non-Jews and possibly needing to have documents. It seemed clear that some system needed to be set up to help them. With the restrictions for foreigners to visit, we'd need another solution.

6

Chukotka's Capital City –
Anadyr

Larissa came to see us off as we eagerly climbed into the small aircraft for the next part of our adventure. She had contacted the pastor by phone so that he would be expecting us. In only a short time we were there – or so we thought. Having collected our luggage out of the hold ourselves, we followed the other passengers, who seemed to be in a hurry. Once outside, we looked around. Other people seemed to have disappeared. Would there be a bus or a taxi into the town to take us to a hotel? How green we were!

A gentleman came along and, in what Russian I knew, I asked about a bus. He rushed off, shouting to someone, who came with an old jeep. We were helped in, luggage and all, and then we set off at a great speed until we reached a wide river. It seemed we had missed the bus and also a ferry. No wonder the others had hurried. After a lot of shouting, our man procured a lift for us in a coal barge, and we were taken to the other side; a journey of about half an hour. We soon learned that the airport is not in Anadyr, but in another place across this wide stretch of water.

The barge landed in what was like a builder's yard. There were many kinds of discarded materials lying around such as heaps of bricks and rubble, old pipes and broken planks of wood. From the barge we had to struggle with our luggage over heaps of stones and bricks and then through the piles of materials. There was no way round. We reached a road but no one was in sight. Apparently there was a bus that came to meet the ferry but we had missed it. We began to pray for help and soon a car came along. We suspected that the coal-barge man had sent for it as the driver seemed to know we were there.

We asked to be taken to a hotel but seemed to arrive at a workman's hostel, occupying the bottom floor of a block of flats. We were soon "booked in" and shown a room with two single iron beds and a shower in a cubicle. It did not take us long to spot the cockroaches… everywhere! There was no food available, but there was a kitchen where one could cook. The only difficulty being that we did not have many supplies. A short reconnaissance outside revealed there was no restaurant, only a small coffee shop selling items like pasties filled with cabbage, potato or onion. Some even had jam in them. But there was nowhere to get a meal, so we made do with some pasties and tea made with our own tea bags and dried milk.

Walking the streets we could see that Anadyr was like Providenya, falling into disrepair, with many housing blocks in a near state of collapse and others very dilapidated. We learned later that much of the population had left because of unemployment and that those lucky enough to have jobs were not being paid.

The governor of Chukotka lived in Anadyr as it was the capital, and was a petty dictator who personally decided who could enter the area, issuing invitations that he personally signed (as he did ours). Even relatives could not come to visit their families without his permission; and there was, of course, a fee to pay of $120 for each one!

~

We made contact with Sasha, the pastor, and had a warm welcome from him, together with his wife Lena. They spoke English quite well – a great help to us. We had to register our arrival in each town so were glad of their help to find the appropriate office. As "tourists", we caused quite a sensation since no such groups ever came to the area. In Russian, we would hear them screech "*Toureests!*" and there was much discussion as they decided what to do with us. They did not have the necessary forms that we had seen used in other places in the fSU, so we had to tell them what to do! Everything was handwritten for us to sign and it was agreed we could stay a few days and also return to Anadyr on our way back. Sighs of relief. Sasha took us to buy our onward journey flight tickets. The next plane would depart in two days' time so we had little choice but to stay for three days.

Sasha told us the church had been started by missionaries from Ukraine. The members seemed to meet in two places and to be mostly people of the Chukchi tribe who were delighted to meet us. It was such a joy to be among them; they were so eager to hear more about the Lord Jesus. As in Providenya, they were enthusiastically reaching out to other villages in spite of the fact that the journeys took days.

The terrain, in our eyes, was impassable and they had five villages to reach. However, despite travelling difficulties, they had already visited four of them, starting small church-groups. The fifth village was miles away and entailed travelling along three rivers to bypass the mountains. They had a huge ex-army truck for winter travel (which came in handy for most of the year!) and could drive straight over the frozen tundra. The enthusiasm of these dear folks was clearly revealed in their bright, shining eyes.

We talked with Sasha and Lena about Israel and the return of the Jewish people, using the Scriptures, which they eagerly received. They explained it all to their church members, who immediately started suggesting the names of people who might be Jews. They certainly knew of a few. The next day we set off to find them. The first was the head of a museum. We would usually start by talking about Jerusalem and how we had been there. For most, this was enough to spark their interest, but the man in the museum was wary. He asked why we were telling him this as he did not want to know about Jerusalem. We told him that people had said he was Jewish, a fact he adamantly denied. We did think he looked Jewish, but he was so nervous we were sure he was just scared. We told him that if he did need help, people were there to assist him. We then had a look around the museum – to please him.

Next we went to the hospital to meet the director, whose name was Moseivitch. He was pleased to meet us; perhaps he thought we were going to donate some money. It was a fact that, generally, people thought we must be Americans, and we heard whispers with the word "*Amerikanskis*" from passers-by sometimes. We started talking about Jerusalem, and Mr Moseivitch suddenly realized why and began to laugh. It was his name. "Oh, no," he told us, "you think I am Jewish! It is just my name. I am not Jewish but I do have someone here in the hospital, the dentist, who is a Jew." He took us to meet Ruslav – a large round man, in a grubby white gown.

In his introduction the director mentioned we were looking for Jewish people, so Ruslav was very pleased to meet us. He most definitely did want to go to Israel and had already sent his wife and son there to live in Haifa. However, he had a very sick, elderly mother, too ill to travel, so he had stayed to look after her. I am sure that by the time of writing this he must have gone.

The next person we were taken to meet was the director of the music school; however, he was away in Moscow. And the last one led us on an adventure. Her address was found in the phone book and it turned out that she was a lawyer. It took time to get there, and the journey had to be on foot as there were no buses. The building was large, well built, and of better quality than any we had previously seen. Up a wide circle of steps we ventured and then inside. No one was about. Highly polished marble floors and stainless steel fittings gave an opulent impression. We studied the names on various doors, including those upstairs, but the name we were searching for did not seem to exist.

We came down again and prayed that someone would come and help us. Almost immediately a lady, laden with papers, came down the stairs. She looked very surprised to see us and very nervous when we asked for the person we had come to see. It turned out that she was the one we were looking for! She took us into a nearby office and appeared to be very anxious about having foreigners looking for her, even more so when we said we were looking for Jewish people and had been given her name. She did not want to talk to us there and kept her voice down very low, asking where we were staying. She agreed to meet us at our accommodation in the evening.

At the appointed time, she arrived, still nervous. The office we had visited was the KGB office and still functioning! No wonder she was nervous! Being so far from Moscow, changes in the way the country was run took some time to filter through. We explained that we wanted to talk to her about making aliyah to Israel. She was interested but assured us it was not for her. Here in Anadyr, she had an important job. In Israel, she would be nothing, making a nought sign with her finger and thumb. No, Israel was not for her. Her mother lived in Moscow and she would not want to go to Israel either, definitely not. She said there were many Jewish people in Anadyr and she would tell them what we had said, passing on the videos and leaflets we had, but she was doubtful any would want to go to Israel. Although the meeting seemed somewhat fruitless she did help us with a great favour for our next journey.

In the morning we were leaving to go to Pevek, a small town right on the shores of the Arctic, and this lady very kindly arranged for us to be picked up and taken directly to the airport, via the barge. This really was a big help and the vehicle proved to be a quality jeep with blankets to wrap in, as the weather was very chilly. It was a great blessing. Sasha and Lena came to our hostel to see us off and gave us a contact in Pevek, another church leader. We said our farewells and arranged to make contact with them again on our return.

Pevek

The return journey to the airport went very smoothly as our driver took charge. He drove very fast and then straight on to the barge. He lost no time getting off at the other end and again drove very fast, directly to the airport – what a difference!

We queued to collect our tickets that we had ordered in advance and then had quite a long wait for the plane to arrive. Apparently flights are rarely on time. We had to carry our luggage through and load it into the hold ourselves, into a space that was quite high up in the side of the plane. It was not an easy task! Fortunately a young man helped me, while Hannah got on the plane to secure seats for us as they were not numbered.

Soon we were off, flying over mountains covered with snow which seemed to get deeper as we reached our destination. This time we were determined not to miss our bus so we hurried along with the other passengers, retrieved our luggage and went out to see what transport there was. There was a bus – well, a sort of bus. It was a small, silver-coloured, very old vehicle, prompting my mind to think of a biscuit tin with windows! It was very full so we had to stand and keep our luggage by our feet.

No one came for tickets, but a lady nearby was obviously very curious about us and tried out her English, asking us if we were Americans. She was astonished to find we were British and lost no time in conveying this information to the other passengers. In any case our Western clothes ensured we were objects of curiosity. Once the bus had creaked its way to the town, this lady said she would show us the way to our hotel, which again proved to be a basic workman's hostel. There was no restaurant, or cooking facilities, so we borrowed two cracked cups and were loaned a kettle for making tea. We had one plastic knife and two plastic spoons left, which soon ended up broken.

Our new-found friend was keen to show us what she said was a beautiful place in her town. We resisted, wanting to explore the town for ourselves, and in any case what, we wondered, could be beautiful here? Pevek was situated right on the Arctic shore, a port for ship repairs and supplies, built by slave labour. Now it was all run-down and semi-derelict, with dilapidated buildings. The coal-fired power station was sending smoke, smuts and coal-dust liberally into the air. It was easily the worst of all the towns we visited!

There was still much snow on the ground, with deep puddles too. The roads, if you could call them such, were full of junk, which had been just left there and which you had to scramble up and over to get past. Nothing, it seemed, was ever cleared up. Eventually we realized this was because for almost all the year the town was buried in deep snow. There were wooden walkways, but most of these had collapsed so we were very glad we had winter boots! It seemed that every walk turned into an adventure.

To our surprise there was, once again, very little in the shops. There was bread and some canned vegetables, pasta, packets of powdered potato and the ubiquitous brown-coloured jam! Vegetables and fruit were a rare luxury and meat and fish very expensive. The small supply of meat we did see in one shop was extremely fatty and smelled awful. It looked like it was only fit for dogs!

~

Back in our "hotel" on the third floor, the beds, with the usual iron frames, creaked badly. To amuse ourselves, we bounced up and down on them in turns, recording the noise! Because it was very cold all the time, the heating was on for which we were thankful, and so, mercifully, we also had hot water for showers. For company we shared the room with the usual cockroaches!

In the morning we were greeted with the encouraging news that there was a restaurant open next door – possibly just for us. However, typically there was only one kind of food, described as *svina cutaletas*, which proved to be rissoles, supposedly of pork origin, cooked in some very greasy gravy and served with thick sticky rice and plenty of bread. "Swine cutlets" became a long-standing joke. Mostly, like the local people, we got by on bread and tea but supplemented this with the "luxury" of a meal once a day in one or other of the restaurants (we had discovered two in the town) – often some kind of mashed potato with unrecognizable meat in a pasty with gravy. Well, it filled us up!

We contacted the pastor, a shy man about 30 years old who welcomed us to his Baptist church, which had been started by missionaries from Ukraine and met in an apartment. The room was beautifully decorated and the lovely people seemed gentle and welcoming. We had a very happy time with them. As before, they were keen to help us, everyone knowing the whereabouts of some Jews, but it took us a long time to find just one.

His name was Leonid, head of the House of Culture, a rather run-down building in need of much repair. He was pleased to meet us and told us he had a brother who was head of the music school, but currently away in Moscow having a rest. He received with joy the photos of Israel, the music, videos and leaflets we had brought. Had he thought of going to Israel, we asked? He replied positively but said, "Not yet". He told us, "I am a big man here and I want to make a lot of money first." We wondered how! He showed us a photo of his beautiful wife who was expecting a baby soon, and then a photo of his little son. He was adamant that he would not go to Israel yet – maybe he would send his brother and his parents who lived in Ukraine. His career seemed to be more important. How could he want to stay in such a dreary, run-down place, we wondered.

He told us he knew of many other Jewish people in the town, some in responsible positions, heads of this and that, and he would share the tapes, pictures etc. and tell them what we had said. We wondered why there were so many Jewish people there – but we were soon to find out.

~

The lady who had befriended us on the bus, and who appeared to be a bit too inquisitive, kept coming to see us and in the end we agreed to go with her to see the "beautiful" place she had promised to show us. We took the bus again – the same battered vehicle which had brought us from the airport – this time continuing along an unmade track to a destination in the middle of nowhere. We could see the sea – the actual Arctic Ocean. My spirits rose, for I had always wanted to be right down on such a shore. *How exciting*, I thought, as we gazed down a sloping bank with rough bits of grass and snow leading to the beach.

As we carefully picked our way, our new friend, Lira, kept saying, "Mind the wires, mind the wires!" We could just see long stretches of old barbed wire mixed in with the rough vegetation.

"What is this wire?" we asked.

"Oh," she replied, "it's left from the camps."

"Left from the camps?" we responded, in disbelief. "What camps?"

She then explained that there had been camps all along the coast as far as the eye could see, right by the seashore. "For prisoners – rapists and murderers of course," she said, "all in Stalin's time." She remembered them.

We questioned her: "All rapists and murderers? Surely not? How could there have been so many?"

She shrugged her shoulders, but it was obvious she did not doubt the information she had been given. We told her a bit more about Stalin and his camps, asking her if the prisoners were perhaps Christians – to which she replied, "Oh, yes."

Then I asked, "What about Jews?"

She replied very definitely, "*Oh yes*, Jews – yes, many were Jews." She went on to tell us that the conditions had been terrible, especially in the long dark winters, with 24 hours of darkness, when there could be a three-week "white-out" when temperatures reached minus 70 °C and there were many blizzards. No one could go out and the cold caused many to perish. The prisoners had lived in wooden huts and had only a stove to keep them warm. They worked in the mines, producing coal, gold, uranium and other raw materials. She said that when the ice on the sea thawed sufficiently, many ran in and drowned themselves; they could take no more. Mercifully it had all ended when Stalin died and Krushchev closed the camps. She seemed relieved. She said that the survivors still lived in Pevek as they were not allowed to go back to their homes, and some of their families had joined them here. So we realized there must be many Jewish people in this terrible place.

We proceeded to the beach where, very proudly, she showed us her *dacha*. We could hardly contain our grins. Usually a dacha is a small cottage in the country with a piece of land around it for growing fruit and vegetables. In Communist times, the more favoured of the people had the privilege of a dacha and some even went to live there so that their children, having grown up, could live in their flats. This dacha was a simple wooden shed, very basic, made from driftwood, though it did have a window. Inside was a small rough table and a bench. It seemed that Lira and her husband, whom we did not meet, plus their family, came here to celebrate New Year, drinking vodka and having a "good time"! New Year in the fSU was a very pagan celebration intended by the Communists to replace Christmas. It had not changed much, in fact!

So this was the beautiful place she wanted to show us! We had to admire it very politely and walk a little on the Arctic shore, where I did put my hands into the very cold water and chose a stone to take back as a keepsake. Our journey had proved useful though and explained why we had seen many people scurrying past who looked distinctly Jewish, particularly in the market area buying food.

We met up with Victor, the pastor, one more time and he told us that the Jewish people did not want to be known as such and had often changed their names and did not hold Jewish services. In fact it was clear that they knew nothing about what it meant to be Jewish. It would be useless to try and call a meeting, for no one would come. We knew this would be a situation needing much prayer. I mentioned that we had not been to a village or met many native people and Victor said he would arrange such a trip as we still had an evening left. It was "'summertime" there and there was light for 24 hours.

It was agreed that we would meet someone at the airport who could arrange transport for us to a village. We assumed we would be going by bus – the usual antique vehicle. However, to our amazement, our transport proved to be a petrol tanker. There were many people waiting, including a little girl, but we had to leave many behind. Four people sat with the driver, two squatted down, and two squeezed between the cab and the actual tanker. We were told that we had to watch for police as we could all be arrested. The pastor prayed for us as he didn't want us to be found breaking any laws!

We bumped over unmade rocky roads across what looked like heather-clad hills, though we could not discern what the actual vegetation was. After a long time, we suddenly stopped. Out jumped some of the "extras" and they seemed to hide among some nearby buildings. In seconds, the police arrived and checked us out – so the pastor had been right to be concerned. We apparently passed the test and were waved on, to pick up the others a little way along the road! There was much laughter at this accomplishment. Eventually we reached another village and were made very welcome in the home of the "mayor".

There were no visions of grandeur here. There was one room, one small table, one chair, and a small, narrow single bed. Several Chukchis (the local native people) were there too, squeezed in already, but happily making room for us to sit on the edge of the bed. They served us a kind of picnic, Russian tea – black and sweet from a borrowed tea set – with some sort of dry biscuits. It seemed this "mayor" was Jewish. He was head of the village plus some sort of accountant, but it was not easy to understand everything and not at all clear if he wanted to go to Israel, or even understood what we were saying to him. They were just so happy to have "foreigners" among them, something unheard of in those parts.

The mayor's facilities were very primitive, the water being obtained from somewhere outside – probably a well. As for toilets, we dared not ask. The house seemed more like a hut, made of wood and tiny. It was quite an experience for us as Westerners used to "mod cons".

It was getting late and suddenly we were told our bus had arrived outside and we should leave. *Bus?* we thought. But amazingly, and as if in a dream, there it was, a white single-decker coach with seats for about 40 people! *Where on earth did they get that from in this village?* we wondered. Soon we were all on and were carried at a great pace back to Pevek. *Why the rush?* we thought. It transpired that the hostel would be locked soon and we were late. It was a little darker by the time we arrived and the bus stopped close to the door, which was soon opened for us. Then we noticed someone peering through the curtains: the woman who had registered us, very suspicious about what these foreigners had been doing. We felt like naughty children out late and we crept inside, after saying our grateful thanks for the adventure. We were a bit concerned for our friends, as it did seem we were being watched. We hoped there would not be any trouble ahead for them. It turned out that we had exceeded the limits of our visa, but that no one had seen the name of the village on the front of the bus.

~

The next day we were leaving so I went to pay the bill. To my astonishment it was for about £50 a night, more than for a top hotel in London at that time. In addition, what food we'd had was extra! I went to remonstrate with the manager. Her considered opinion was that the bill was fair.

"After all," she said, "look where you are staying!" Apparently, she put her town on a par with a top tourist resort.

I told her it was more than we'd pay in the Hilton in London. She didn't seem to be impressed, doubtless because she had not been anywhere to know the difference.

After I assured her that we were pensioners and could not pay such a price, she softened a bit, though she questioned how, as pensioners, we could afford to travel so far from England. It was impossible to tell her the truth – that we walked by faith and the Lord supplied our needs; she would never understand, so I said we'd had to save for a long time and friends had helped us. In the end, she gave in, and simply because we were pensioners, said she would reduce the bill to about a third of what she'd originally asked for. To me, it still seemed a lot for creaky beds, cockroaches, and cracked crockery!

It was hard to say goodbye once again to our new friends, who waved us off as we left on the antique bus to the airport. We were to board another small plane, again loading our own luggage into the hold, heading off for another adventure – this time in a place called Bilibino. What would we find in a place with such a strange name, we wondered.

7

Bilibino

After landing, we again found the airport to be a bus ride away from town. Thankfully, this time the bus was a newer and better model! We were also taken to a real hotel too, which was a pleasant surprise after the working men's hostels in the other places we'd visited on this trip.

The hotel was clean and bright with significantly better furniture and beds. Alas, there were again no eating facilities; just a borrowed kettle and more plastic cutlery. We wasted no time going outside to explore. This time we had no pre-arranged contact to meet us as the Pevek pastor did not know anyone in Bilibino. However, the Lord, of course, does know each of His people in every town and He made the way for us quite unexpectedly.

Looking around, we could see mountains in the far distance, which were covered in trees on the lower slopes, giving the appearance of autumn gold. It was the end of August and winter would not be long in following. The first snows actually started while we were there – on September 1st. The wind was very strong, making it hard to stay upright, and the cold reach of its fingers was felt right through all we were wearing. Even our thick anoraks were not adequate, but that is the nature of the weather in the Russian Far East. It was a sombre reminder of the suffering the prisoners went through in the Gulag camps.

However, despite the chill in the weather, Bilibino proved to be the nicest town we visited and for me about the only place I could call attractive, of all I have ever visited in the fSU. It was very clean because of an atomic power station outside the town, way up in the valley. (Every year since the Chernobyl disaster, this power station was checked by American scientists and hence the hotel was of a reasonable standard.) The radiation level was displayed above the Cultural Centre, along with the time and the temperature. We could see this from our hotel window. In a way, it was reassuring.

Here, as everywhere else, we were a great novelty, with people staring at us and eager to talk to us. "*Toureests?*" they'd say, in great wonder, asking, "Which delegation are you with?" They found it hard to believe we were not with an organization. They'd never seen anyone from England and assumed we were American. Some would stroke our sleeves in amazement as if we were from another planet. In a way it was quite fun to walk the streets with the people so friendly. The whole place felt better somehow.

We were looking to buy some food and were surprised to find a few more shops. One sold clothing of reasonable quality, and shoes too. There was also a baker and we joyfully bought a loaf, which was still warm. The assistant was very interested in us and spoke a little English. Then, wonder of wonders, a food store with actual food in it! We tried out a type of cream cheese and bought some biscuits, little cakes and tins of carrots and peas; quite a feast after what we had been used to! There was also a little teashop of sorts where we treated ourselves to a cup and a rather tasteless little pasty.

It was while we were in there that a lady approached us shyly, asking in a mixture of English and Russian if we spoke English. Then she explained that her husband would really like to meet us. She did not say why, so we were very puzzled. How could he know about us? We agreed he could come to the hotel the next morning at 10.00 a.m., simply because she was so eager and friendly.

Before retiring for the night, we had a prayer time as we were a little unsure about the man coming to see us. The next morning he was exactly on time and proved to be a good friend and a big help. The lady in the baker's shop had told this man's wife about the English-speaking people, which was why she had come to find us. He was an enterprising English teacher called Alexander who taught a small group of children using an ingenious method he had devised himself. Each of the children he was teaching became a character in a story about elves. Alexander was eager that we might sit in on one of his lessons and also speak with the children. We were delighted to agree and he took us to his home that same morning to meet the group of children. These youngsters were having great fun and were really doing well learning to speak English, even though they were a little shy to speak to us at first. We were very impressed with them.

Alex told us about the governor of Chukotka who had wanted to be the mayor of Bilibino as well as governor of the state. He had failed to gain the vote and as a punishment had deliberately hindered anything that might help the people to prosper. For example, Alex told us that he himself had tried to get a tourist programme started with ski runs, log cabins, river trips and the like. It was to be a joint venture with some Americans investing the money. We could see the possibility of this since the mountains nearby would attract people. However, the whole project was crippled by this governor, resulting in Alex losing his job.

An additional punishment imposed by the governor was a ban on hunting – thus cutting off the people's main supply of food. The result was that many had become poachers instead! Here, as elsewhere, there was a great deal of unemployment, little by way of wages and little for the ordinary people to eat – only the mafia and businessmen did well and they were 10–15% of a population of about 6,000 people. When walking the streets, this was not really obvious, and certainly the people seemed to be better off than those in the previous towns we had visited. Maybe because it was cleaner and looked better, social problems were not so apparent.

Alex had started his English teaching as a means to earn a living and managed to survive on what he earned. He told us, "We even have a little church!" and asked if we would like to go, although he himself did not attend. If we wished, he would take us and introduce us to the pastor. He said that the church had been started by missionaries from Ukraine. And so we were introduced to a Pentecostal church which has its own building but not really many members. It was the older style of Russian Pentecostal, keeping rigid rules, most of which applied only to the women. They had to wear longer-style dresses, and were never to cut or dye their hair or wear make-up and jewellery. Also, married women were expected to have a baby every year (because James wrote that a woman is saved in childbirth! They did not realize that James meant "protected" during childbirth). Thus the women had to cope with many children while being very poor.

In this church, women sat separate from the men and were not allowed to speak from the front, so neither were we! However, we had good conversations with the *three* pastors, who proved to be very keen to help us find any Jewish people.

There seemed to be few Jewish people around, but maybe they were hiding their identity. We found two very poor families that had no documents and so could not prove their Jewishness. In one of them was a lady called Olga who was a believer and a member of the church. She was married with a ten-year-old daughter called Sasha (also a girl's name) and had a terrible story to tell. As a child she had lived in Firenza, a city in eastern Russia, and was exiled to Magadan with her mother, father and three sisters. They had lived in a wooden hut along with many others and just had a curtained-off pair of bunk beds between them. Their father was sent to work in the gold mines and their mother had to work too. The children were left alone with little food, always cold and hungry. Sometime later their mother contracted and died from TB because of the terrible conditions, and the rest of the family were sent back to Firenza where Olga's father brought up the children by himself.

When, years later, Olga wanted to get married, a KGB agent suggested she pay him money to get her papers altered to say she was a Russian Gentile rather than a Jew. She agreed to this for safety more than anything else. Her husband eventually died and a second marriage brought Olga to Bilibino. She was desperate to go to Israel and asked if we could help her. She gave me some photos of herself and her sisters (with whom she had lost touch), along with their names, and I promised to take them to the Bureau for Lost Relatives in Jerusalem in case they could trace any of her family. We suggested she go back to Firenza to search the archives, but somehow she did not want to do that – I think she was afraid for some reason. Also it was unlikely that she could afford it. The family had very little money and out of any she could save, she used to buy one apple a week for her daughter. Such poverty! Nevertheless, as is often the case with poor people, Olga insisted on sharing her food and making us a meal. Someone had killed a moose, which is a very large animal, and so the meat had been shared between many people. Olga had a piece of this meat in her fridge and unbeknown to us had cooked it for the meal she prepared for us! She explained what it was and we pretended we were not too hungry, eating only a tiny helping so she would have some left. What precious people these were!

In Jerusalem, much later, I did leave her photos at the Bureau for Lost Relatives and they made great efforts to find Olga's sisters but unfortunately were not successful. The people at the bureau agreed that Olga's sisters looked very Jewish, but even so, they would need real documentary proof. I sent the photos back to Olga but have never heard from her to know if she received them or if she did try to get documents from the archives in Firenza.

~

A man from the second family we found came to Olga's home to meet us. He looked gaunt and very hungry. He told us that his father had registered them all as Russians, having suffered so much himself for being a Jew. He would not agree to change this registration, even though he knew his son wanted to go to Israel. He was much too afraid. We did not meet the father or any other Jewish people there and were not really able to help either of these two families, other than raise prayer for them, which we did later.

Olga said there were other Jewish people in the area, probably among the scientists working at the power station and research centre, and said the church people would contact them for us. One of the church members worked at the research centre and informed us that they were monitoring all the atomic tests that took place in the world. Any Jews there would undoubtedly find it exceedingly hard to get permission to leave, even if they did want to go to Israel. They knew too many secrets!

One morning we were stopped in the main street and interviewed by a lady journalist. She kept asking what we did not like about her town and her country. She was very persistent. We avoided direct answers and said truthfully how much we loved the people and how different it was, which made the area very interesting! How could we mention the dirt, the mud, the decay, the cockroaches etc.? The townspeople did not know it was unusual to have dirty, foul-smelling water in which to wash yourself, or toilets which constantly needed adjusting to make the cistern work (I became quite expert at this!). We didn't dare mention the "hotels", with grimy windows which either wouldn't shut or wouldn't open, and dining rooms with no food. She seemed pleased enough with what we did say, though.

~

When the time came for us to leave, Alexander took us to book our flight back to Anadyr. However, we discovered that the disgruntled governor had stopped these direct flights. Instead we would have to go back via Pevek, and flights were only once a week. (They also apparently went this way from Anadyr to Moscow.) The only other route was to go south to Magadan. With a flight to Pevek only once a week we would have to stay for two extra days and that would make it difficult to get back to Anadyr. The major problem was that the flight from Bilibino arrived in Pevek after the flight to Anadyr, which would mean waiting there for two more days. Then the flight to Providenya arrived in the afternoon, too late for the midday flight to Nome with Bering Air, which had been arranged for us. If we missed that, we'd be stranded until someone booked a charter flight with two spare spaces which we could ask to take. If we did that, we would then be too late for all our connections back to England! Oh, it was so complicated. We all prayed for a solution. Somehow the mayor heard about us and suggested we go by helicopter direct to Anadyr as one was scheduled to go, providing the weather was clear. That raised our hopes, but the weather was cold, cloudy and the sky filled with snow, so eventually this idea came to nothing.

On the day of our chosen flight we set off for the airport, a grey, gaunt building with no chairs for passengers, a stone floor, no food or drinks available, and a pack of dogs running in and out. Although we had tickets, we were told there were no spare seats for the incoming flight, which was very late. It was Monday, and to make our connections we had to be on this plane. After stopping at Pevek, it would go on to Anadyr from where the next flight to Providenya left on Wednesday. If we didn't get this flight, the next one was a week away! We simply had to get on it. The cold reached into every corner of the airport and we prayed we would get seats on the plane.

At last the flight arrived and, to our amazement, we were called forth first and ordered to bring our luggage for weighing, which was amazing as we were actually well back in the queue – if you could call it that. We were then sent through, carrying our bags to hoist them into the hold. It seemed there were four spare seats and we were allocated two of them. It was a wonderful answer to our prayers – praise God! However, there was more good news to come. Our God is so amazing! On our arrival in Anadyr there was no sign of the plane to Providenya, so I went to ask about the time of the next flight, just in case the one for that day was delayed. At the desk I was informed that it would be tomorrow, Tuesday! I thought the lady had misunderstood me and asked her again. I told Hannah, who said to check once more, as it should be on Wednesday. The lady was understandably irritated by my third request and she flung the book around to show me – yes, the next flight was tomorrow, Tuesday. "*But no tickets!*" she roared at me – in Russian.

Puzzled at the change of date, we thought maybe it was today's flight delayed. Then we remembered – we'd needed to get to the ferry but had missed it! We needed somewhere to stay the night, or we would have to sleep in the airport somehow. On enquiry we found there was a place and, joy of joys, it was a room with two spare beds. The Lord is so good to us; He promises to take care of us and so He does. We found a place to buy the ubiquitous cabbage-filled pasty plus a plastic cup full of a brown liquid that was difficult to identify as either tea or coffee. We were too hungry to care and later had a reasonable night's sleep.

Being on site we took encouragement in the fact that we could be in good time for our flight. We prayed for tickets and again approached the desk. "No tickets," came the reply. We waited. The flight was late coming in from Providenya. We waited and waited. In any case if we did get tickets at the last minute, the plane would get back to Providenya too late for any flight to Nome. We were booked on Bering Air for that day and the planes usually left at midday as this was the only time they could fly because of the weather.

We had plenty of time to pray – and so we did and trusted the Lord to get us on the flight. We were at total peace, certain we would be on the plane. And we were! At last it arrived and we were called forward because, mysteriously, two seats had become available!

The flight took about 45 minutes and we reached Providenya at about 2.30 p.m. As we came into land we were amazed to see three Bering Air planes in the area designated "International Flights". Our plane was late, and usually Bering flights arrive by 2.00 – 2.30 p.m. at the latest, while the light is good enough. It was after 3.00 p.m.

now and we had expected there would not be a flight for us. We desperately needed one in order to be in Anchorage for our ongoing flights to the UK. We had one day left and had been thinking we would have to ask our friend in Anchorage to change our tickets for us. We wondered what was going to happen.

We left the plane and, with our luggage, went through customs, exiting the domestic part of this tiny airport. From outside, we had to go back in by some steps to the international area! There were no airport officials around. None at all. *Where is everyone?* I wondered. Puzzled, we prayed what we should do. Maybe we should phone Larissa to come and help us. There was a phone on the wall between two doors, but a queue of passengers had formed to use it. I leaned on the wall near to the phone where one door was slightly ajar. I could hear voices from within the room and suddenly one voice exclaimed "Esther! You are here!" It was a lady from Bering Air whom we had met a few times. She invited us in to where a group of rather tough- looking men were sitting. She explained that they were fishermen just ending a cultural exchange. There were 16 of them, but their boat had been held up by the tide and so they were late.

She went on to explain that they were planning to fly at 4.00 p.m. and they had two spare seats – would we like them? "Would we? Most definitely." What an amazing God we serve. He had delayed these fishermen so that we could fly with them. Amazingly, too, the weather had remained clear with a bright blue sky and sunshine in evidence. In no time we were all on board and flying back to Nome. We had not eaten all day so we hoped to get something in Nome where we would have to stay the night, since the Alaska Airlines flight would have left much earlier. There would be one in the morning direct to Anchorage, but we still might need to change our ongoing flight back to the UK.

Our Bering Air friend, Teresa, was overjoyed to see us. She had received a message that we were on the plane so was eagerly awaiting us. She told us, "I have booked you on the flight to Anchorage." We asked about staying somewhere overnight – but she interrupted to say, "No, there is a flight this evening, leaving at 9.30 p.m. Alaska Airlines sent an extra one up today and it is outside. I don't know why, but it is here." Teresa went on to say that she had contacted our friend in Anchorage who would meet us to take us to her home. Again we were awed at what God had done! It was just amazing. He had changed times and flights for us. The other thing we had forgotten was that in travelling to Chukotka, we had arrived a day and one hour earlier since we had crossed the International Dateline. Now we had returned, gaining a day and one hour. So we suddenly had a spare day. It was like a gift: time to relax and sort ourselves out.

In the airport, there was no water, no facilities for tea-making, and no food available either, so we just had to be hungry. We did not say anything; after all, how could they help us? Soon after nine o'clock, we boarded the Alaska Airlines plane. It felt warm and cosy after our chilly adventures in Chukotka. The stewards came along with drinks of juice and little packets of nibbles. I asked them if they had any other food since we had come from Russia and had eaten very little all day. The two stewards looked at each other and went away. Soon they returned to explain that when they had flown up to Nome, they were supplied with meals for the passengers, which was most unusual. They did not know why because it only takes an hour's flying time. However, two people had not wanted their meals so they were available! The steward asked if would we like them. Hallelujah! They asked us to sit at the back where the fishermen would not see us, as they had no meals to give them.

Soon we were tucking into large rolls with tasty burgers and some salad too. They also brought us more of the little packets of nibbles plus some souvenirs – pilots' badges and the like. They wanted to know about life in Chukotka as they only landed in Providenya, no further. We felt very cared for. Our God is so faithful and He does provide for all our needs – and in unexpected ways.

~

Once in Anchorage, our friend Barbara met us and whisked us to her home. It was so wonderful to sleep in such comfortable beds after a hot shower in clean water. Barbara washed all our clothes in a huge machine and dried them in another so we could pack everything clean and sweet-smelling. Our spare day flew by and soon we were off to Seattle and Chicago where we could share our findings, before flying on to London and home. Everything back on schedule – all done by the Lord's Almighty Hand.

8

Back to Chukotka

*O give thanks unto the Lord; for he is good: because his mercy
endureth for ever.*

(Psalm 118:1 kjv)

Having been back in the UK for a short time, Hannah and I met to
pray about returning to Chukotka. We felt that although we had met
a few Jewish people, we had made little headway in helping them
to go to Israel as there were so many problems. Firstly there was
the question of documents proving their Jewishness. Many people
were survivors of the Communist camps and no longer had papers,
having destroyed or lost them. To search the archives meant long
journeys to the cities from which their families had come and most
of them were barely able to survive on what finances they did have.
Then if they did have documents, they would have to go more than
once to either Khabarovsk or Moscow to see someone from the
Jewish Agency and an Israeli consul.

These were difficulties indeed but the problems went deeper still.
The Jewish people knew only that they were Jewish. They knew
nothing more as there were no rabbis, no synagogues, no Jewish
communities where they could get together, and no Jewish Agency
either. Nothing. They were the most hidden Jews we had come
across. It seemed like "Mission Impossible". We really felt we should

go there again. First, though, was the problem of getting permission to go in again. The Lord did it for our first visit. Did He want us to go again? We wondered if perhaps one of us could stay out there to set up an office in Anadyr, the capital of Chukotka. So many thoughts were in our minds.

At about this time (late October 1997), there was an article in The Times stating that the Russian government might have to evacuate all the population from the areas of the far north. Chukotka and Kamchatka were mentioned, and the town of Pevek in particular. It stated that there was insufficient food and fuel for the winter. Where all these people would go was not mentioned and, since the winter there is nine and a half months long, what would happen to their homes and belongings while they were away? Would they later be allowed to return?

Our enquiries from a contact revealed that the people knew nothing about their government's plan. Was it just speculation – or was it God's way to get His people to a place where they might have access to finding documents? We were puzzled – and very concerned as the people had had very little food when we were there. How were they managing right now, we wondered. More than ever, we felt we must go back. We felt sure this was the Lord's plan.

~

In February of the New Year, when the Bering Air office opened, we contacted our friend there to ask advice about applying again. She encouraged us, sending us the appropriate forms which we duly returned. Later, when requested, we sent the necessary $200 each for our papers to be examined. We heard nothing. Weeks went by. Then, as a result of our repeated enquiries, early in June we received further forms to complete and return. We were told the situation looked "hopeful". However, we felt it all needed a push in the spirit realm because we needed to go while it was summer there. The flights with Bering Air began in July and mostly ended in September when the snow began again – usually about the 8th. It left us a narrow corridor, with all the delays in getting permission. Besides we needed to get flights across America, wait in Seattle for our visas (if we did get permission), go on to Alaska and wait there for a charter flight with spaces for us. Our times are in God's hands as He has so often proved. Nevertheless, we felt led by the Lord to fast on alternate days for two weeks. We began on June 29th, finishing on July 13th. We found it harder to fast like this, but persisted to the end.

Miraculously, we received permission three days after having finished the fast! We were not given permission this time for all the towns, but just two – Providenya where the planes land and Anadyr, the capital. This latter was essential. What an amazing God we serve. He did it again – and at a time when it was increasingly difficult to get visas for anywhere in the fSU, let alone for those restricted areas where foreigners were not welcome!

We felt impressed by the Lord to stop off in Chicago and Seattle en route, as well as Anchorage in Alaska. This was to give us opportunity to meet people who could help establish contacts and thus a route for Jewish people fleeing from Russia, via the USA. How much longer did they have, we wondered, as things were increasingly deteriorating over there and the Jews at that time were being blamed. We needed teams to meet them and to look after them. In hindsight, this all seems a bit premature, but at the time it was very real.

We booked our flights to Chicago where we had a contact, and onwards to Seattle where we would need to get our invitations processed into visas. We had new contacts in Seattle and would need to meet them during the three days it took to do the visas. We could book our flights on to Anchorage and Nome, but to cross the Bering Straits to Chukotka we would need to wait until someone chartered a plane with two spare seats that they'd be willing to sell us.

Our visas were for three weeks, finishing on August 31st. Timing was crucial because we would have the same problem returning – the need for spare seats on a chartered plane returning in time for us. At the time we were travelling, no one had chartered planes either way!

I love situations like this, for God is faithful, and when He wants something done He sets it all up. We do need to pray though, and our faithful prayer partners were all alerted to "stand in the gap". And this they certainly did, for God answered those prayers and arranged everything!

We set off to Chicago on July 27th and on to Seattle two days later. In both places we met people who were very enthusiastic to support any Jewish families able to set off for Israel via the US. They were thinking way ahead for the days when the "hunters" would come (Jeremiah 16:16) and the full exodus from the "land of the north" would begin (Zechariah 2:6). God had been giving specific prophecies and visions relating to this exodus and we were thrilled to hear about them. These American believers had thought of many forms of transport, but notably motor homes, since a route had been set up by the government from Alaska along the west coast of Canada to what they called the "mainland" (of the USA) with camping points equipped with electricity and water. These motor homes would be ideal for helping families, we thought. However, visions from God often have to await an appointed time (see Habakkuk 2:3), as we realize today, since we are still awaiting the exit of Jewish people from the Russian Far East via the USA and Canada. What is exciting is that Ebenezer now has a representative in Chukotka working with the churches and organizing ongoing prayer both in the Russian Far East and in Alaska for the release of the Jewish people. God is at work and His timing is perfect.

~

For our return journey, we booked to fly from Seattle to Chicago and then to London on September 8th, reasoning this would give us time to report back in Anchorage and even perhaps have a day or two spare. Hannah provided help for the new churches as well as for the Jewish people in Chukotka – books, teaching materials, as much as we could carry, and we both had financial aid too. The poorer Jewish people had no funds for obtaining their papers, let alone food. We were wondering if God wanted an office set up in Anadyr and that was why we had been given three weeks on our visas. Would there be time to do it perhaps? We'd need to find the right person there, someone who could encourage the Jewish people to get their papers. It was quite an awesome thought.

We obtained our visas in Seattle with no problem and booked our return flights on Alaska Airlines with a stopover in Anchorage. Here we stayed with our friend Barbara for a few days until we heard there were two seats available for us on a flight from Nome. At last we were off. It is quite something to fly over the Bering Straits in such tiny planes, seven- or nine-seaters. Our luggage was either under our feet, or under the wings! We always had to wait to be sure the weather would be clear, as it often was around midday. The planes did not fly high so we had good views of the sea and often spotted beluga whales frolicking in the blue waters. The approach to Providenya meant we suddenly turned right and almost immediately came onto the landing strip right at the edge of the sea. It always seemed we would land on the water!

Our luggage was quite a size, two bags each, and we wondered what the Russian customs officials would say. Last time they had been so amazed we had tourist visas and a route inland they did not open our bags. This time we had much more. However, they were more interested in how much money we had! The man carefully counted what we allowed him to see and then waved us through, even helping to carry some of the bags. He was very cheerful. Amazing!

Providenya revisited

This time we were met by our pastor friend, Larissa, who welcomed us into her home. The situation was even worse than it had been last year when we were there. The same governor was still in charge, as much of a despot as ever. He refused to accept humanitarian aid for the people, saying they did not need it, while we found the people struggling to survive each day. They lived on the fish they caught, plus berries and mushrooms from the tundra. During the short season without snow, they would walk for miles to gather wild foods – and then eagerly want to share them with us! What was worse, though, was that the coal-powered energy plant, which supplied the town with hot water and central heating, had broken down. The result was that people had been heating their homes by burning rubbish! Also the water pipes were blocked and broken so there was no water in their taps. They had existed throughout most of the winter like this. We were amazed at their ways of managing.

To obtain water, people had pushed the bottom ends of plastic bottles into the crevices of the mountainside where water was coming through. This caused the melted snow to go through the bottles like a constant tap running. You may remember that in order to build blocks of flats, ledges had been cut into the sides of the mountains and the flats were built leaving a path behind each row. It was here behind the flats that we could obtain such water.

While staying with Larissa, we went to fill buckets with the water pouring out of these bottles. With this we filled her bath and other vessels, thus providing ourselves with water for every purpose. The water was brown and we had to strain it through four jars of cotton wool and then of course it had to be boiled, but at least we could wash and make drinks! As it was "summer" and not quite so cold, we kept warm enough in our woolly winter gear. Larissa explained, "We are survivors here", and laughed it all off!

Back in Anadyr

The weekly plane to Anadyr was due and amazingly had two spare seats so we did not spend long in Providenya. Larissa contacted our friends, who eagerly met us in Anadyr. They had found a flat for us to use; it belonged to a church member who had gone to Bible school in Moscow. It was only one room, but empty! Just an ancient electric cooker in the kitchen, much of which did not work, and an old sofa in the living area. Our friends soon rallied round with a fold-up camp bed and some blankets for us; also mugs, plates, spoons and forks. They only use large-type carving knives, so we were not given any table knives! An old kettle and a pan completed our equipment. From the window, we had a view of the waters where an enclosed netted area had been set up for trapping fish. It entertained us a great deal when we were there to see seals slipping over the edge to dine on the fish!

The other less welcome creatures were the cockroaches which appeared while we were out and covered every surface of the kitchen so that it glowed with a golden sheen! There were hundreds of them, simply hundreds. As we came in and banged our shoes on the top of the cooker they would disappear in less than seconds! It was amazing. Yuk.

We found minimal food supplies in either the market or shops; mostly it was foreign and very expensive plus the usual tins of peas and carrots and some bread, but there was no meat, cheese, fruit or vegetables. The governor had taken the subsidy off bread so a small loaf cost the equivalent of £2. We wondered if the intention was to drive the Russians back to the mainland and let the natives starve.

But God was very much at work in this bleak, desolate place where grass, flowers and trees were an almost unknown blessing. We met again our dear Christian brothers and sisters with their shining faces, along with many more believers, so much had the churches grown. They eagerly evangelize everywhere, especially in the outlying, almost inaccessible villages. We heard wonderful stories of how people came to salvation and of God's many miracles of healings and provision in times of great need. For example at a meeting earlier in the year, one man had died of cold and hunger. He had no pulse or heartbeat, yet two of these dear new believers prayed over him for more than an hour and he was raised from the dead. He soon gave his heart to Jesus and lives now to tell the story – we met him and heard it first-hand.

God really met our needs in that He put the right people in the right place at the right time. It was truly miraculous the way He set everything up. Last year we had found a small Pentecostal church in Anadyr and their leader had begun to find the Jewish people. This pastor had gone back to Ukraine for a rest and was replaced by a young man who spoke really good English – such a help to us! He had already made good contact with Sasha, the other leader, and between them they had located over 300 Jewish people living in the town.

In addition, there was a third new church, very charismatic, only a year old yet already with over 60 members. We went to meet them, taking some of our literature, videos and audio material etc. This new group were shouting "Hallelujah" at each item as we showed them. No one else had supplied them with anything. Now there were three churches and, before long, God had them in unity, reconciled together with joint services, holding hands and praising God together. It was wonderful to see. We learned that each church had been praying for this unity and also for a way to help the Jewish people in the town. Wow!

The three leaders asked us to teach their people, from the Bible, all about Israel and God's plans and purposes for His people. We also taught those who felt called to be "fishermen", with the direct result that there was a group ready to reach out to the Jews in love and to help them go to Israel. The very next day they were bringing us news of people they had found!

We had gone there feeling that God would do something more specific this time and He did. The Jewish people there are more hidden, more afraid, more unaware of what it means to be a Jew than any I have met anywhere else. It is not surprising, since most are relatives or descendants of those from the camps or exile in this former part of Stalin's Gulag. Many have changed their names, lost their documents and have no proof they are Jews. They just know it – and they look it too. We often spotted Jewish people along the roads; it sometimes seemed we were in Jerusalem! However, we knew we could not call for a meeting. They simply would not come – not if foreigners invited them. To put up a notice suggesting they come to a certain hall at, say, 10.00 a.m. on a certain day would frighten them off immediately. Our friends assured us of this.

Foreigners were rare in this closed military zone and we were stared at wherever we went. Some did pluck up courage to speak to us, but in the main, people were still wary. The KGB was still active there and we were told, "They know everything." Our friends reported how, after we had left the last time, the KGB had visited them to ask why we had come and what we were doing there. They were very suspicious so we knew we had to keep a low profile as far as the Jews were concerned.

We realized it would be better, as a strategy, for local people to visit the Jewish people to share about the possibility of going to Israel. Pastor Sasha had recently rented a building which the believers used as their church. It had other rooms, one of which he used as an office. He very kindly offered to make a space in it for someone to work on behalf of the aliyah. We prayed together about how to set this up. One man in his team agreed to be responsible for helping the Jewish people. We'll call him Pavel. He planned to gather just a few to start with and to teach them about being Jewish. He would ask to use a room in the Cultural Centre and help them to celebrate the feasts and, since Rosh *Hashanah* (Jewish New Year) was soon, he hoped to start with that. It is a fact that Jewish people know others and have their own ways of passing on information. He felt he would soon have others join his group.

It began to be really exciting. We gave them money for expenses or to help any Jewish people wanting to travel to get documents, or to see a consul. This was from the wonderful finance sent to us by believers in the UK anxious to help. We arranged a way to send more if and when needed. Sasha now had a fax machine so we also worked out a code for sending messages using numbers of fish when referring to Jewish people. For example, if we said, "We netted 20 fish today", it meant that number came to the meeting. Or "Bought seven fish" meant that we spoke to them about aliyah. We also taught them the various routes used by the Jewish Agency and Ebenezer, at the same time encouraging them to look out for any who would be willing to travel through Alaska.

Since we had two weeks there, we thought we just might get permission to go to Pevek again. Sasha had taken us to register our arrival and to check seats on planes back to Providenya. However, when we found the dates of planes, we realized it would be impossible to go any further inland since flights only went once a week. We hadn't enough time. We had to go back another day simply to see if there were any seats on a Providenya flight in time for us to get back to Nome and complete our itinerary back to the UK. We still did not have seats on a charter flight to Nome, in any case.

As there were no seats available on the next flight to Providenya, we were told to come back again to ask about the next flight – the last one possible. The days were going past and our visas expired on August 31st so it was essential we had seats on this last flight. Using Sasha's fax machine we sent messages to raise the prayer level.

~

In the meantime, we had wonderful times of fellowship with the three church groups. Obtaining food was a challenge. Usually we just ate bread and vegetables from tins unless we were invited somewhere. People always wanted to share their meagre supplies with us; it was very touching. One day there was a loud knocking at our flat door. Outside stood a small girl, aged about 7, carrying a large plastic bag in which was a whole large fish – a salmon – and a big carving knife. It appeared she had walked right across the town, alone, to give us this fish from her father who had caught it. We were deeply moved. We had no means to cook it, so we took it to our pastor friend Sasha, whose wife Lena agreed to cook it for us and share it with others. She made quite a dinner party with it – delicious!

We also met again some of the Jewish people we had contacted the last time we were there. Although we had encouraged them to go to Israel, using the videos, music tapes and Scriptures, we discovered that the lady who had them, the Jewish lady from the KGB office, thought they could be propaganda of the sort the Soviet system put out. The videos showed life in Israel – the beautiful fields, the full shops overflowing with produce, the beaches; everything that would make people eager to go. Because of this, she had not passed them on although she was friendly enough towards us. She was adamant that she would not go to Israel herself, preferring to go to Moscow instead, if she went anywhere. She gave us a gift – a small icon as used by the Russian Orthodox Church. It was a carved wooden picture of a saint to whom we should pray! We were polite and thanked her, of course.

~

We decided to go again to check for available plane seats, only to be told the plane was full! What could we do? We prayed as always, and as always, God made a way as only He could. Our Jewish lady wanted to say goodbye to us so we mentioned the problem to her. She phoned someone and said to leave it with her. She arranged for us to be taken to the airport by her driver the next day, in a jeep, which was of better quality than normal, complete with warm blankets. She gave me an envelope to give to the airport manager and wished us luck as we went off. "Just give it to her!" she called out as we drove away. It was great to go in the jeep straight on to the barge, crossing the river and on to the airport without trying to catch a lift.

Once in the airport I asked where I could find the manager. Hannah stayed with the luggage as I was directed up some stairs where I knocked rather timidly at a door. A large blonde woman looked at me, snatched the envelope and without opening it screamed, "Casha, Casha!" at me. I must have looked puzzled, but she waved me back down the stairs and I realized she meant the desk where you book tickets. The woman there took one look at me and foraged under her table. She brought up an old cardboard shoebox which she rifled through, lifting a lot of papers until she found what she wanted – tickets for foreigners! Smoothing out two of them, she wrote something in Russian and demanded payment (I have forgotten how much) and handed me two tickets for the flight, scowling at me all the time. On reflection, we decided they must have cancelled tickets for two other people in order to let us on the plane – giving foreigners priority. Our Jewish friend must have ordered them to do that. It did seem that the KGB still had influence. Our God does get things done and He certainly works in mysterious ways too.

Soon we were on the plane to Providenya – but wondered if there would be a flight to Nome with spare seats for us as well? We really needed one that day so that we could be in Anchorage in time for our flights back to the UK. This flight was on time so there might just be a Bering Air plane...

We arrived in Providenya – no planes. We went out through the doors from the domestic side and back into the international entrance, which sounds so grand. We asked at the desk about the plane, to be told it was on the way, delayed by the cloudy weather, which thankfully had now cleared.

The customs officer also greeted us, eager to know how we had spent our money! "Souvenirs?" he enquired. We laughed because there had been nothing to buy, but we said the hotels were very expensive, which could have been true had there been any! He believed us and let us through. Soon we could see our tiny plane approaching. Watching it land we prayed there would be two spare seats for the flight back. The Lord always has it in hand and sure enough there were two and we could have them!

Soon we had boarded and were on our way back to Nome, arriving in time for the flight south to Anchorage. We now had one night during which our clothes were washed in a huge machine and tumbled dry ready to pack the next day. Everything worked exactly on time for each of our flights back. We stopped to give a report in both Seattle and Chicago so that our contacts could be ready should any Jewish people manage to travel through from Chukotka to Alaska. Then it was on to Heathrow and home!

~

It was only a few weeks later that we learned about our first Jewish family to go to Israel, but not via Alaska – not yet. Pavel, our man seeking to help the Jewish people, had somehow found a family in a desperate situation. They lived way out in one of the villages. The mother had died and the husband had no work. There were three young children. Pavel was appalled. They had no food except a stale mouldy piece of bread. There was no heating and they had hardly any clothes. He wondered if they were Jewish; they were and had papers to prove it. Pavel wasted no time, bringing them immediately to Anadyr where he found people to care for them while he sought advice as to what to do next. The Ebenezer Office team in Khabarovsk suggested he brought them all there, which he did. Once there, they could meet the Jewish Agency representative and later the consul who dealt with their application to go to Israel.

The Ebenezer team in Khabarovsk provided them with clothes and took care of their every need. Soon they had their visas and were off to Tel Aviv. They were so happy! Much later, we heard that the man had married again and everything had turned out well for them. Praise the Lord, for His mercies endure for ever!

9

The Chukotka Story Continues – the Third Trip

Having arrived safely back in the UK, Hannah and I prayed into further possible trips to Anadyr. Would the Lord send us again? We knew the situation there was dire and, as the next winter came and went, we heard of various agencies such as Samaritan's Purse, the Red Cross, etc., getting some food supplies to the suffering people. Through a friend, we were able to establish contact with a man from Alaska who went regularly to Providenya. He was able to take finances in for us and also messages out. During this time we also heard of some Jewish families or individuals who chose to make aliyah. They either went via Magadan and Khabarovsk, or via Moscow. We were able to fund some of their travels through the finances sent in. It was all very rewarding, yet so far no one wanted to try travelling via Alaska.

By February/March (1998) we decided to apply to go back to Chukotka once more. We soon hit a problem – our past avenue in had closed as our friend had left her job to have a baby. Her replacement did not speak Russian and lacked the expertise to push through for us. We were given another name but it took weeks of sporadic contact to finally establish the fact that he had done nothing, except to say he would do something! After this we found a third contactwho seemed more confident. We prepared all the papers and again waited. Amazingly, the visa invitation arrived very late on July 31st. Knowing it was on the way, we booked our flights, only to discover we had been given just one town – Providenya, where the plane lands near the coast – and no further way inland to the capital Anadyr where all our team were. It would be like landing in Dover with no permission to go further. It was useless.

For 24 hours we wondered whether to push on in faith but had no conviction to do so. We'd been given only two and a half weeks – not enough time to go there, get permission for Anadyr and get back, with flights being just weekly. In any case we had no definite booking either way with Bering Air. We cancelled our flights, and arranged for more funds to be taken in for the team to help more Jewish people go to Israel. We realized we were in a spiritual battle needing much more prayer and thus we took time out to do just that.

We raised the level of prayer support and continued whenever possible to send finance to help our friends in Chukotka. Then, for some time, we heard nothing except that food supplies were very low. Nothing was being sent in from Moscow. *How on earth are the people existing?* we wondered. Time passed, and less and less news came through.

In the meantime, however, the Lord sent Hannah and me for some very interesting spiritual warfare journeys both in the Middle East and across Russia. Through another friend, we were given a contact for Russia who was a member of the Russian Parliament – the Duma. His name was Vladimir and, for a fee, he obtained a multi- entry visa for us. We were allowed to choose three cities, but when we mentioned Chukotka, he froze, telling us not to mention that place. His work in the government was in dealing with humanitarian needs and he had already made us part of his committee without us knowing and we agreed to supply clothing and shoes. We did some journeys into Russia this way for a year or more and each time this man met us and found us accommodation, as we arrived with huge bags of supplies for him. He was a wonderful help.

The Lord was very much in all of this. During the second year Vladimir asked if we wanted to renew our multi-entry visas and hinted that he might be able to get us into Chukotka. It turned out that Putin, who was the Russian prime minister at the time, had appointed a new man to be the governor of Chukotka and things were changing there. Nearly two years had flown by and we longed to go back. Somehow, Vladimir obtained permission for us by way of an invitation to Anadyr, which was exactly where we wanted to go.

~

Back in the UK, we lost no time setting up the journey. It was the end of May, early for such a trip, as the Bering Air flights would have only just started and we did not want to waste time. We had only a month. Maybe we could get permission to go on to Pevek and Bilibino. Would that be possible? We really hoped the Lord would open the doors for us. Then we could come back through Providenya to Nome, thus meeting all our contacts. This was our thinking. How wrong we were!

We set off on May 28th, flying with KLM from Amsterdam via Vancouver to Seattle and on to Anchorage. Here we would wait until there was a flight from Nome to Providenya. Our friend in Nome was back from maternity leave and eager to help us. She said there might be a flight out on June 5th, but for our return trip several were available in late June and would fit in with our timing. It all looked positive.

We had no idea what we would find in Chukotka. We knew that there had been very little food or heating, and many old people and babies had died. This much had filtered through. We also heard that the new governor was more caring than the previous incumbent and had plans for the region. His name was Roman Abramovitch, sent there by Putin to revitalize the region, and amazingly he was Jewish! He was also very rich, having made his fortune in the gas

industry, and later on became well known in the UK as the owner of
Chelsea Football Club!

~

When we arrived in Anchorage, we caught a flight to Nome,
ready for ongoing travel on June 5th. In Nome we found out that
our next flight had been cancelled! The only possibility now was
on June 12th – another week of waiting. We knew the Lord must
have a plan and, in seeking it, discovered there would be a Summit
Conference in Nome for June 13–14th between Chukotka and
Alaska. It was for delegates from Washington, Moscow and
Vladivostok, as well as Chukotka and Alaska. They were to discuss
ways for mutual co- operation in economy, trade, transport, oil and
gas exploration, tourism, education and so on. We were amazed and
felt we were there to pray about it all. We learned that on June 12th,
three Bering planes would be going to Anadyr to bring 27 delegates
to the conference, nine people on each plane. We could go over in
one of the planes direct to Anadyr! It seemed just great.

However, this created an unexpected problem. We thought we
would only need one night's accommodation in Nome but now
needed a week. It seemed that delegates for the summit had booked
all the rooms. Here again, we found that God had a plan. Through
the relations of a friend's friend, we were offered the use of a house,
the owners being away on holiday. Not only did this save us heavy
hotel bills, but more importantly, gave us the freedom to spend time
in praise, prayer and proclamation, which we did daily.

Sometime before, we had had a vision of a bridge between
Alaska and Chukotka. It was golden like that in San Francisco, but
was not joined in the middle. Somehow, it seemed the conference
decisions would be an outworking of this vision of building a
bridge. We used many Scriptures to lay the right foundations,
for example Micah 6:8, Matthew 12:25, Luke 6:46–49 and Isaiah
35. We prayed for the right people to attend, for right attitudes,

motives, openness, unity and so on, and for everything to be under God's guidance. We were reminded of that Scripture verse in Psalm 127:1: "Unless the Lord build the house, they labor in vain who build it."

The venue for the summit was to be a former church building, now a community centre. We prayed inside it, including upstairs on a balcony, and many times circled it outside. Meantime, we were preparing to leave on the 12th.

To our dismay, we discovered that we needed further documents to be allowed into Chukotka, having previously been assured that our visas issued by the Russian government were sufficient. Now apparently they were not. We did not realize at that time that our visas did not include names of towns where we had permission to visit. Nome may be in the USA but we faced innumerable problems trying to send faxes from there or to make international calls. A major block was the time difference. Everyone was in bed when we were up, and in Anadyr it was always the next day – across the International Dateline! Urgent messages to England raised the prayer level and the Lord prevailed. From England a message reached our Moscow Duma friend, Vladimir, who made contact with the new governor of Chukotka. Through this, we were able to contact his secretary who promised to do everything for us. Talk about friends in high places! It was just amazing. We wondered if they knew what we were doing.

We eventually received oral permission to go to Anadyr but by now we were too late for the June 12th flight. God had us in Nome for the two days of the summit, so we were still there to pray it through. We felt there was a joining of the two sides of the spiritual bridge, yet on each end was a gate which was closed. All this was seen in spiritual visions. *What is God doing?* we wondered.

The return flight for all 27 of the delegates was on June 15th and it appeared that there were no seats available for us. However, again God had a plan. Some delegates decided to stay on for a few more days and suddenly there were spare seats, room for us!

Oh, were we relieved. It was a lovely flight with superb views of snow- covered mountains and frozen seas. At last, with great relief, we reached Anadyr – joy of joys. However, again the joy was to be short-lived – we were not allowed out of the airport! We had no papers, just oral permission. Our visa invitation, it seemed, did not count without permission to enter the city! After a long delay, our verbal permission was checked by phone, which really did take a long time.

At last everything was agreed and we were sent by helicopter along with six or seven construction experts from Canada. They had been brought in by the new governor to build safe homes and new schools and hospitals. It all sounded amazing. We were taken safely over the still, mostly frozen estuary, into the city, where we soon met up with our lovely friends. What a welcome we received! They had waited so long, patiently enduring all the different changes in dates and times. They had come to meet us and it had seemed we were not on the plane. Even then they had waited. Bless them.

We had much to share amid hugs and tears of joy. They soon had us settled in a flat where we could plan our days. We had insufficient time now to think of going on to Pevek or Bilibino as we had spent so many days in Nome. In any case we learned that internal flights had been cut to the minimum and then unpredictable weather could be the cause of delays. It was still early in the season, hardly "spring" yet and very cold. We just had to settle for Anadyr and then Providenya. The next news was a shock too – there were now just weekly flights to Providenya, the next one being on Tuesday. It was already Saturday evening. That meant we had only two more full days in which to do everything. "Help us, Lord!" we prayed. And He did.

The three churches had arranged their Sunday services to be morning, afternoon and evening so that we could be at each and meet all our old friends. We had time to hear their stories and to get an update on the "fishing" work. What a precious group they were, still working and praying together, teaching the new churches about

Israel, seeking out the Jewish people, giving them help where needed – all we could have hoped for and more.

The whole atmosphere there had changed; the extreme sense of heaviness had lifted, replaced by a cheerful air of hope. These people had cried out to the Lord in all their depravation and hardship and He had heard them. The harsh conditions, lack of food and heating in the winter, the terrible weather – nothing had stopped them from serving the Lord. We heard how they had gone with dog- sleds in the depth of winter taking help to outlying villages often 16–19 hours' journey away, much of which they would walk as the dogs did not have enough to eat and were exhausted. They told their stories with big smiles and radiant faces, making light of their difficulties. There had been nothing in the shops for over a year, not even soap, they said! They had to catch fish or sea mammals which they shared – everybody shared. None of their church people had died but many had fainted. On two occasions humanitarian aid had reached them from Samaritan's Purse (Alaska) who delivered it to them personally.

They told us how the people had given money for the Jewish work when they heard about Israel and what God was doing in these days, regathering His people to the Land. They so wanted to be a part of it that they gave out of the little that they had, a total of $1,500. They were still sending from the tithing in their little churches to support the Aliyah Fund which we had set up. They told us, "We bless the Jewish people and now God is blessing us."

And this was how God blessed them. Their new governor, Roman Abramovitch, instituted changes for these dear people in ways that were quite amazing. Abramovitch was Jewish, young (in his thirties), extremely wealthy, having made his money in gas, and he seemed to have taken these people to his heart. On his first visit to Chukotka he saw appalling poverty. So the first thing he did was to send every person, from the oldest to the youngest baby, a huge food parcel containing everything they could need: flour, sugar, rice, spaghetti, bulgur wheat (kasha), powdered milk, oil, tea, powdered egg, salt, tins of meat, condensed milk – and many other items. It saved their lives. For some there was hardly room enough in their tiny flats to store it all! We heard that he paid for it himself, but that was not confirmed. In addition he arranged for everyone who worked to receive their correct salaries and for any wages that were overdue to be paid promptly. No wonder the heaviness had lifted!

Another amazing thing he did for these people was to send every school-age child for 45 days' holiday at resorts on the Black Sea. He even sent mothers with the younger children. In these resorts were old sanatoria from the Communist days where members of the hierarchy went for rests. The children were sent to stay in these places where they also had medical checks (there was much TB around) and dental treatment. Abramovitch also arranged for each of them to have new clothes and shoes. What a great heart he had! We actually saw a planeload of children set off, waving cheerfully to their happy parents. We were shown newspaper pictures of them playing in the sea; these children could never go in the sea in Chukotka. We also saw a picture of Abramovitch on his first visit to Chukotka, realizing the extent of the poverty. His face was a study of concern. The headlines said it all: "We love you, Roman." This was not surprising. God had truly heard the people's prayers.

Besides all this, we learned that Abramovitch had bought new helicopters for the villagers to use – lovely bright blue ones. Also he was having a new international airport built for Anadyr and was setting up new international flight programmes. There were also plans for new roads and resurfacing of existing ones, which was much needed. Nowhere had we seen such potholes and terrible surfaces. Abramovitch's programme was transforming the whole area.

Sasha told us that it was now considered something positive to be Jewish and that the formerly frightened, hidden Jews were beginning to come forth and admit their ethnicity. The work of encouraging Jews to make aliyah was still slow, however, as the people knew little about what it meant to be Jewish and had problems with documents.

However, a few people had gone to Israel during the years we had not been able to get in to Chukotka. The team had done a wonderful job and had begun to assemble people in the Community Centre where they could learn about Jewish history and culture. They even had had a Passover meal with their new supplies of food, and 15 people had attended. The idea was to awaken their hearts to their Jewishness so that they would long to go to Israel.

We had just left that day and were on our way to buy tickets to Providenya when we hit another problem. We were not allowed to buy tickets because we did not have a document permitting us to travel there! Off we went to the governor's office to try and sort out the problem. Unfortunately, Mr Abramovitch was away (we would have loved to meet him) and we had to content ourselves with speaking to his secretary. We did not recognize the previously drab place; it was totally transformed. The entrance was filled with huge boxes of electronic equipment – computers, fax machines, printers etc., all being unpacked and carried inside. A young, enthusiastic team of "yuppie" types were employed and were not allowed to smoke or drink alcohol. Even Roman Abramovitch, we were told, didn't smoke or drink on the premises. Gone were the drunken, extravagant house parties of the old regime. Praise God!

Inside, the place had been decorated and painted pastel shades; it was truly beautiful .We then met the secretary, a young, attractive, friendly person, very smartly dressed. She was pleased to meet us. She told us not to register, but if we would wait, our permissions would be ready within the hour. Another lady downstairs recommended that we went to the airport that evening as the weather forecast was not good. She herself booked us into the hotel at the airport, and then presented us each with a book about Chukotka – but all in Russian!

We rushed back to Sasha's to finalize things there and then went back to the ticket office where all afternoon we waited, but alas the permission did not come. In the end we had to pack in a hurry and go across the river by barge (the ice had just thawed enough) to get to the airport. We had no tickets for the flight, but this had happened so many times to us and God had always made a way. What would happen this time, we wondered.

The ticket office was closed and we knew we might not get tickets in the morning. We did not even have time to pray before a voice behind us said, "I hope you have a good flight!" There was the second lady from the morning who had advised us to come early. We told her about our situation and in minutes she had got the ticket office re-opened, being all indignant that it was closed! We were sold tickets without any questions being asked about permission! What a wonderful God we serve. He put the right person there to help us, exactly the right person. We had a really good night's sleep.

Sasha and some of our friends came to make sure we got through customs without any problems, and then we were off. An hour later we were in Providenya where we could see Larissa through the fence, smiles on her face. She waited for us to come through as we usually did, but this time the customs and border guards were present. They wore uniforms like policemen and had guns in their belts and took us into a small room for questioning. It seemed we had no permission to be there! How many more times could this happen? We were asked many, many questions and were kept there for four hours, while sets of forms were completed by hand, four copies of everything! Then we had to write statements about what we had done. We hardly knew what to write and they could not understand how we had got there. According to them we should not have been allowed on the plane – we had broken all their rules but we did not know how! They were very insistent that we had no right to be there and would not phone to Anadyr to check that we had been given oral permission. We told them that papers were being prepared. They were intransigent and did not want to know. In the meantime we grew very weary, hungry and thirsty as the hours ticked by.

Eventually they allowed us to go, having told Larissa that we should report to the military base the next day to complete another paper. Dear Larissa spent much of the next three days trying to get us registered, always smiling and calling us "Girls"!

Eventually, we were given up to eight days there, after which we must leave. At that point it did not seem too much of a problem.

Little did we know!

~

We spent the days with Larissa attending the church where she was the pastor, and joining in with their prayer meetings and worship. We also took time to pray and make proclamations as we had done in Nome, using the same Scriptures, and praying for this side of our "bridge". We felt God was doing something significant because of the way He had kept us for these extended times each side of the Bering Straits.

Larissa told us of two Jewish people, a mother and son, who wanted to go to Israel – and they lived at the top of her block of high-rise flats. It was a special treat to us to go up and meet them, although they were a bit wary at first. We answered their many questions about Israel, which encouraged them. Their major problem was that they had lost their internal passports, which everyone had, and needed to get replacements before they could get international ones and apply for visas to Israel. They had sold all their furniture and were living in just the tiny kitchen, using camp beds. Our team representative in Providenya had been helping them with money each month and would take care of their travelling needs. We were able to add to this and bless them with a financial gift from those who specifically gave for such purposes. Although they had been wary and really a bit shy, they ended up hugging us, as we shed tears together. They would have to go all the way to Moscow to finalize their papers, and then fly to Israel from there. We did not hear any more of them but believe they did get to Israel in the end.

It was very cold and damp in Providenya with a lot of snow still around. The power station that had broken down was being repaired thanks to Abramovitch, who had provided the finance, but for much of the winter the people had once again been without heat and often without electricity. We had our warm winter clothing and were only there for a week, but *they* were still smiling at the end of the winter, making light of it. They were amazing people. The water pipes were also being repaired so water was in short supply and therefore there were no baths for us; we declined the offer of the sauna!

Although the shops did have food (more than we had seen before and brought in by plane) we found out that a large ship was on the way with extra. This was good news, plus the food which Roman Abramovitch had provided ensured that no one was hungry. Larissa made her own bread with flour from a huge sack and using a bread maker she had obtained from Alaska. It was delicious. We seemed to live on this bread and also on chips as every day Larissa cooked us a panful!

~

Having been allowed to stay on, we still had a few days left so decided to check the means of our departure. It came as a shock to discover that Bering Air no longer came to Providenya which explained the lack of planes when we first arrived. They were now going direct to Anadyr which meant we would have to go back there. That proved impossible because all tickets had already been sold, as had those for the next plane from Anadyr to Nome. This scenario seemed to be the common characteristic of the trip. "Help us, Lord," we prayed, wondering how He would solve this one.

Larissa had a friend in Nome who she thought might be able to help, but there was the problem of time zones. It was Saturday night for us, but Friday for Nome and the Bering office was closed for the weekend. We managed to get a message through to our friends in England via Larissa's fax machine to raise the prayer level. All calls went via Moscow, even to Alaska, which seemed crazy to us as our messages to and from England went halfway around the world, but also right round the world to get to Nome – and Nome was only 30 miles away!

Later on Sunday evening (Saturday in Nome), Larissa managed to get through to her friend and explained the problem. She suggested we call a man called "Jim" who she thought might have a solution. She gave us his number and after several tries we made a connection. It was 10.30 p.m. when we called him and it sounded as if we had woken him. We explained our dilemma and he was very encouraging and helpful. It seemed he was something to do with Bering Air so our plight was of legitimate concern to him as we were two of their prospective customers stranded in Providenya. He assured us he would do something to help.

The days passed but not the uncertainty we felt about our situation. The weather was awful. We waited, we prayed, we phoned. We heard it would take up to three days to get permission to land in Providenya. We also needed the weather to clear. We heard there would be a plane on Tuesday but later found out that it had been cancelled because of the thick cloud. We really did battle in prayer. Then on Wednesday, about midday, gaps appeared in the clouds and our spirits rose. We went to the airport, scanning the sky as it brightened. Then we saw it – a tiny plane coming in! It arrived – a small six-seater, not the usual big plane that goes to Anadyr, but it seemed as if it was sent just for us! We could hardly believe it. The Lord is good!

In no time at all we were through customs and on board, where we learned that "Jim", our contact in Bering Air, was actually the director of the airline! We had indeed woken him up with our call and, being genuinely concerned about us, he had sent this plane, using a trainee pilot and instructor, especially to pick us up! We were just filled with joy, hardly believing we were up in the air on the first leg of our journey home. What an amazing God we serve. He certainly does open doors no one can shut.

~

Back in England, a few days later, we reviewed this strange journey and what we had achieved in the time: ten days in Nome, two in Anadyr and eight in Providenya. We had seen our teams, had a clear update of their work and their financial situation, and heard their plans. They had a representative in each town with finance to assist the Jewish people, who were slowly choosing to go to Israel via Moscow or Khabarovsk. They were giving humanitarian help where needed, searching out new Jewish contacts and teaching about Israel in their little churches. It was all very encouraging.

But what else had God been doing? He had caused a spiritual bridge to be built, with closed gates, which we did not understand except that it seemed it was not yet the right time for the Jews to go to Alaska that way. He had supernaturally cut through all the red tape which kept people out. We had gone in, travelled about, and come out again without one of the so-called vital documents we had been told we had to have; not one. None were ready in time. Everything had been by verbal permission from the governor's office – something unheard of.

Then what about the planes? Each time, there hadn't been any tickets or seats and we had no permission, yet each time, miraculously without questions, tickets were available, seats spare... God was surely at work. Since returning to England we learned that the new governor was changing the rules so that it was possible to go to Anadyr and Pevek with just a visa, no other permission being necessary. He also had plans afoot for scheduled flights from Alaska and a ferry in the summer when the ice had melted, linking the islands. We heard it had been suggested that there be visa-free travel for residents of Chukotka and Alaska between their two territories. It was all mind-blowing. There was no end to the possibilities – but we did not hear any more of this. Was it fulfilled or was Abramovitch replaced before it all happened? We do not know.

Gradually, over time, we had less and less contact from our friends in Chukotka. Maybe once a year we would manage to get through, or they would reach us. They always had good news of church growth but little about the Jewish people. It seemed God had it all on hold until very recently when Ebenezer Emergency Fund began a work establishing teams in Russia and Alaska, with a representative in Chukotka. There were plans for prayer actions and more besides. "The vision awaits an appointed time" was true for Chukotka and Alaska.

10

A New Season

Enlarge the place of your tent,
And let them stretch out the curtains of your dwellings;
Do not spare;
Lengthen your cords,
And strengthen your stakes.
For you shall expand to the right and to the left...

(Isaiah 54:2–3a nkjv)

The Lord made it very clear that I was to start travelling worldwide to find Jewish people, encouraging them to make aliyah, and to teach in the churches about the fulfilling of God's prophetic word in our day. He sent me to many countries and often things were straightforward so I will mention just the highlights. Others, however, involved exciting events, for our God is an amazing God who opens doors into seemingly impossible places and makes ways when there seem to be none.

South Africa

The first place I visited was South Africa where I actually went twice, including Namibia. At the time, the crime rate was extremely high so there was strict security everywhere. I managed to set off the alarm twice where I was staying, bringing the armed guard within a minute! It was not safe for me to go outside alone, either walking, by bus or taxi, so I was carefully looked after everywhere I went. I was interviewed on television by Trinity Broadcasting Network (TBN) and also for a Christian radio service, which in itself was amazing as anti-Semitism is rife due to the belief that Israel practises apartheid. I was asked appropriate questions and was able to reassure them that there is no apartheid in Israel. The broadcasts go throughout the country, so God used this means to combat error.

There was a good response in the churches since at that time most did not know much about Israel or what God was doing. People were very excited. The highlight in Cape Town was a meeting to which I was invited to speak to the *Bnoth Zion* (Daughters of Zion). These were ladies from Jewish groups who had come into town for the day as they did once a month. We met in the huge Jewish Centre. I don't know who was most moved – me, at the privilege of talking to them, or they, hearing how God was bringing His people home and why He was doing it. I showed them slides of the Ebenezer work in the fSU which they loved. *But...* they did not want to go; they felt no need. I told them the time would come and they should be ready to listen for God's command. I left them with a plea not to leave it too late and they were nodding in tearful agreement.

As part of the second trip, I went on to Namibia, which used to be German West Africa. This is very obvious from the architecture in the capital city, Windhoek. Because of the anti-Semitism, no church responded to the request for me to come and share. My friends there arranged two small meetings in their home and I was also able to share a little at a ladies' prayer meeting. One good thing was that a prayer group for Israel and aliyah started and they were eager to read the books and watch the videos that I had brought. Then I was invited to meet the local Jewish community who were celebrating Purim. They number only 45 in all – and that included the little children and a baby! They were very suspicious of me and not at all interested in aliyah until one of them spoke up. She had just returned from working on a kibbutz and she waxed enthusiastically about life there. They listened to her because she was related to one of them, so maybe there's a chance some of them did finally go to Israel.

In Johannesburg, I was invited to lunch at the Jewish Centre where there is a residential block for the elderly plus a large hospital and medical centre. The mesh security around it was as high as a house with security barriers at the entrance. It was obvious what kind of situation these dear people faced, and the fear they lived with. I was made very welcome by cheery ladies wanting to know all about what I did – but once again they made it clear it was not for them! There were very elderly Jewish folk there who had survived the Holocaust and had Nazi numbers tattooed on their arms. Some told me of loved ones they had lost in death camps; others that they had been in prison camps set up by the British on Cyprus during the time of the Mandate. This act of the British made me feel so ashamed I wanted to hide under the table. I tried to express my feelings, shedding tears, and left them touched, but for me it was not enough. My heart ached. They did not want to go to Israel at that time, but in recent years there have indeed been several flights from South Africa bringing Jewish people to Israel; some with help from the Ebenezer team. Praise God – He has His timing.

India and Burma

My next journey was to India and to Burma (today called Myanmar). First stop was Mumbai and then Madras (now Chennai). India was just like we are told: crowded, hot, dusty, colourful and noisy with people living in unspeakable conditions and every imaginable form of traffic. There were Hindu shrines and temples, tiny shops and street stalls – and plenty of mosquitoes. The villages had small thatched homes with wells for water, no gas or electricity and no real roads. Everywhere there were crowds and children going barefoot. My heart ached – so many millions trapped in idolatry and their leaders closing the door to the gospel in many states.

It seemed there were no laws restricting religion in Mumbai, where I was able to speak freely at specially arranged meetings. The pastor who set it all up for me went on to spread the message of aliyah as he headed up "Spirit-filled Churches of India" which meant it went far and wide – praise God! In his local congregation was a man involved with the local Jewish community where he had much favour. He took me there for lunch. They were the most regal, elegant-looking Jewish people I had ever met – taller, pale-skinned – and were very gracious. They told me they had been DNA-tested and it was found they were the direct descendants of Aaron, that is, they were the *Cohanim* or priestly line. There were about 3,000 of them in Mumbai and were known as the *Bnei Israel* (Sons of Israel).

We talked about their going to Israel. I was told that many had already gone, part of a steady flow at that time. In the beginning, the Jews from the villages had returned to India because they found they could not fit into Jewish society after their backward village- style life. So in order to prevent this, the Jewish community had set about educating and training them, especially the young people. This meant they were able to get jobs and settle down. *What wisdom*, I thought.

Chennai was different. There were no known Jews there – they had all gone to Israel already! As in Mumbai, the Christians were touched by the message of Israel. It was new to them and they were eager to start to pray. However, here, the new laws against Christianity were being implemented and a man from America, on a tourist visa, who was speaking openly in the churches, was arrested, beaten up (some said he was also stabbed) and thrown out of the country. I praise God that He kept me hidden because I was also openly speaking in churches and also only on a tourist visa. My host, a pastor, was eager to disseminate the teaching about Israel and the return of the Jews to all his churches so that prayer would be raised up everywhere. It was very rewarding.

~

My next stop was Yangon (Rangoon) in Myanmar. At the airport were several businessmen and as we waited for our luggage one of them questioned me. "Are you part of a group?" he asked. When I confirmed that I was alone, he looked concerned, drew a card from his pocket and said, "If you have any problems, contact me. My name is Stewart." I had not thought that going to Burma might be a problem! I had had to book a guide and a driver so over the days I was there, I was "looked after".

I came to an agreement with my two helpers – "No temples or pagodas" – and I also told them I would walk around by myself some of the time to enjoy the "people". We visited a park, a lake and the zoo; things were very limited as I would not go to temples. Once free, I set off from the hotel with the map my guide had given me. Downtown Yangon had narrow streets on a grid pattern. There were crowds, much rubbish (mostly old vegetables) and people sitting and eating at small tables along the roadsides.

A thin man approached me. "Do you want Moses?" he asked. I guessed he meant a Jewish man. How did he know I was looking for a synagogue? I saw from the map that it was somewhere in the area. It never ceases to amaze me how the Lord puts the right people in the right place at the right time! He led me around some streets and there was the synagogue, evidenced by a large Star of David in the metal of the gate. A man inside saw me looking and he too asked if I wanted Moses. When I admitted that I did, he said to come back the next day at 10.00 a.m. as Moses was out – a good start!

The next morning, Moses was waiting for me – an Indian man but obviously Jewish in his looks. He was so pleased to have someone to talk to in his excellent English. He told me that only eight Jewish families remain in Yangon and they do not come to the synagogue. All the others had gone, mostly to Israel. He had three children and he planned to send them to Israel to marry and then return and re-establish the community! Well, man can have his plans... I knew that once in Israel, his children would not want to go back.

We talked about Israel but he did not want to go there; after all, who would look after the synagogue? No, he had to stay and look after God's house. He would not be persuaded otherwise. The synagogue was beautiful and very well kept. I shared Scriptures with him from my Bible, which he thought was a prayer book. It became obvious he had never had a Bible. I offered to send him one, but he froze in fear as religious books are not allowed to be imported. Praise God my case had not been searched as I entered the country! It was full of Christian literature and items for the Jews. He showed me a chest full of old, dusty Tanachim (Jewish Old Testaments). They were in Hebrew which he could not read, but he was amazed I could – and translated what it said at the start of Genesis. He obviously longed for the Word of God to read for himself. I promised I would get him a Bible somehow and said I would come back.

Returning towards my hotel in the hot, hot sun (45 °C), I prayed earnestly to find Christians so that I might do the job that God had sent me to do. A minute or two later, a man stepped out of the crowd on the right. He was wearing a light-blue shirt with a large white cross on the left side. I said "You are wearing the Cross of our Lord Jesus Christ!" In seconds we were talking and I learned he was an elder of a Full Gospel Assembly, that they pray for Israel, and that the pastor would be delighted to meet me. What a faithful God we serve. It was an instant answer to prayer.

As a result of this meeting, I was invited to speak to four different congregations about Israel and God's present-day fulfilment of prophecy to bring His people Israel back to their Promised Land. They all loved it. The pastor also gave me a contact in Mandalay where I was to go next. It is true that if we trust the Lord He makes a way. I had arrived in Burma with no contacts, but the Lord had gone before me and set up everything!

~

Mandalay was quite different. It had mostly unmade roads that were dusty and with no identification signs. They were set out in a grid pattern, which meant I could not have found my way as they all looked alike. Added to that, the street lights went out at five o'clock, leaving everywhere pitch dark. I was grateful that again I had to have a guide and a driver. With potholes, ditches of murky water, lumps of concrete and general rubbish on the road, I would not have felt safe walking the streets. My guide and driver looked after me very well.

Before I went to Burma, I had learned that in north-eastern India and over the Burma border lived the Chin tribe who had been identified by their lifestyle and by DNA as being the lost tribe of Manasseh. Today, Israel is bringing these people back from north-east India and they are known as *Bnei Manasseh* (Sons of Manasseh). But my trip was in March 2003 and the decision had not then been finalized. I really hoped I would meet some of them in Burma. Well, I did – in Mandalay!

The pastor in Yangon had given me the contact details of a pastor in Mandalay so I went to find him and his church. I met his wife, Luna, who told us that the pastor's brother had just arrived from the US where he leads a church of Burmese people. God's timing in this only impacted me later on. I met Pastor Khai from Tulsa, Oklahoma, and he listened as to why I had come. He invited me to his conference, which was starting the very next day, and offered me a slot to share with the people!

We got there early. My guide and driver were excited that their guest was to speak! I discovered that most of the congregation were of the Chin tribe, now truly born-again believers in Yeshua. They were all excited at the idea of going to Israel. Their belief that Yeshua was Messiah could herald problems for the aliyah as the Israeli Ministry of Absorption would not consider them as being Jewish any more – viewing them just as Christians. It would have to be the Lord that sorted that one out! However, our God is God of the impossible, so we must pray He fulfils His word and He will bring them home. At the present the Bnei Manasseh are only being taken from India.

Pastor Khai asked me to send teaching material on Israel to him in America, as he planned to make it part of a course in the Bible school he was to set up in Mandalay later. The Burmese authorities will not allow such materials to be sent in by mail, but God has His ways and His timings. If I had gone to Mandalay earlier, I would have missed meeting Pastor Khai! As soon as I returned to England, I packed a parcel of teaching material for this Burmese pastor in America, which would later be used for the church in Mandalay. What a wonderful God we serve!

I had also been given the contacts for a bishop and an orphanage run by his church. He listened carefully and with great interest, as I talked to him about Israel and the present ingathering of the Jewish people. He also gave me a Bible for Moses which he signed for him. He was a very gracious man. We were introduced to the children, who sang for us, and also those in another orphanage. I had funds to share with them too, for which they were most grateful.

~

My guide wanted me to meet his wife so he took me to their home. I was shocked. It was one in a line of tiny one-room dwellings, each about 8 x 6 feet. A fence separated it from the road, with a narrow yard in front. Inside was a small table with a wooden bench behind it, on which his wife sat. *Where do they sleep?* I wondered. By the front door a wooden plank sloped up under the ceiling with a thick rope dangling which enabled you to pull up on the plank, which then led to an 18-inch-high area with a mattress on the floor. It was their bedroom. *What about a kitchen?* I asked myself. That was easy. Outside in a corner of the tiny yard was where they cooked. It was a triangular area with a cover fixed on the two side walls. Two bricks formed the base and they used bits of wood and rubbish as fuel! What if it rained, I thought. They seemed unconcerned at the problems the weather might throw at them. And as for washing facilities and a toilet, apparently there was something at the back – I did not go to see!

It seemed that Shueva (my guide) wanted me to pray for his wife to have a baby! That was apparently why he had brought me to his home. Well, I was happy to do so – but how on earth would they f it a baby into this minute home? I did not ask. I prayed and trusted the Lord to answer and maybe they would come to know Him in His time.

We had eaten at various "restaurants" – all outside and all by water, which meant there were endless numbers of large mosquitoes ready to pounce. Also the food was labelled but not really recognizable as beef, pork, chicken, or fish. I was reliable informed later that it was more likely to be "cat, dog, rat, or monkey". I am very glad I did not know this at the time! Praise God I was never ill.

~

Back in Yangon, I kept my appointment at the synagogue to deliver the Bible. Only Moses was there – there were no other people and no service. He was overjoyed to have a Bible in English for himself. He kept kissing it and promising over and over to read it – all of it. I knew he would too.

I had to return via Bangkok, Thailand, and had a day between flights. I arrived late at night at an excellent hotel where I was able to relax and sleep late as I was very tired. Later I felt impressed by the Lord to book a river trip. I was to get there by bus and asked the Lord where I should sit. I felt Him urge, "Second seat from the front". I was used to Him guiding me in small things and by experience knew He had everything in hand. Across the aisle I could hear a young couple speaking Hebrew – they were Israelis. What a finish to my journey. We spent most of the trip on the boat, discussing the situation in Israel at that time and where their hopes lay. I shared with them God's plans for them, told them how much He loved them and that they needed to put their trust in Him. They were a lovely couple, eagerly taking in everything. We hugged warmly on parting.

What an adventure I had had. I could tell so much more. Even travelling on Indian trains and Burmese buses would be a story in itself. I had met Jewish people, and I had spoken in churches as well as with individuals about God's plans for Israel today and the importance of Jewish people making aliyah. To Him be all the glory.

Singapore, Australia, New Zealand

Having heard from the Lord that I should "go to the nations", I was not surprised when he directed me to Singapore, Australia and New Zealand. I had always wanted to go to these places but the main problem was that I only had one or two contacts, so how could I set up a trip? In those days, Ebenezer did not have offices there, just some representatives. However, some of my friends knew people in these nations so via emails some plans were made.

I must say at this point I did not have a computer, having persistently refused to have one. How obstinate can one get? Seeing that I really needed to answer the emails myself instead of my dear friend Marilyn undertaking it all, I repented before the Lord. I prayed that if I should have one, He would give me a small computer as I had no money to buy one. No one knew any of this. Two hours later a man phoned me about an article I was writing for a magazine which he edited. He said that it would help if I put it all on a disc. "Disc?" I queried. Whereupon he said he understood that I did not have a computer but said he had a small one that he could give me! How about that for an answer to prayer? Within an hour he arrived.

It took time for me to learn how to use it and since then I have had others, including a large PC, but now years later I have a smart new laptop and would not be without one!

~

It was September when I set off with one definite meeting arranged in Singapore. Then as time went on, I had five booked there, plus one definite and one "maybe" for Australia and the same for New Zealand. All in all I was away for six weeks and clocked up 45 meetings in 22 venues – in churches, halls, homes, large groups, small gatherings, as well as in synagogues and Jewish gatherings. It was just amazing and all glory goes to the Lord for it. People I had never met welcomed me, cared for me and simply wrapped me in their love!

In Singapore, besides the meetings (where the people eagerly listened to the message), I was taken frequently to the markets where we seemed to try every kind of Chinese food. They joked that their diet was "See food and eat it!" I am really surprised that they stay so slim. I also learned to use chopsticks as there was no other way!

Then I went to six cities in Australia altogether – Perth, Adelaide, Sydney, Melbourne, Brisbane and Rockhampton. In each I ended up having three or four meetings at least. In Melbourne, we had the most meetings, one of which was with the ladies of the Jewish organization "WIZO", because the local Ebenezer lady had a great relationship with the Jewish community. We gathered in the home of a very wealthy family where the kitchen was just enormous. They had a huge TV on one wall from which we could show a video about the ingathering of the Russian Jews by ship from Odessa to Haifa. They loved it and asked many questions.

I gently began to talk to them about the Lord's call for the Jewish people to go home to Israel. They were very quiet as I told them that surely their time will come for them to hear Him and be ready. They nodded their heads slowly, obviously thinking about it, because even then there was a rise in anti-Semitism and they knew it. It would have taken some real shaking to move them though, because they were so comfortably settled there in Australia and Israel did seem very far away.

In New Zealand I had many meetings, but the most exciting thing was meeting many young Israeli tourists. Having finished their army stint, they were having a break, travelling abroad to recover from all the tension they had been enduring. A Messianic Jew had made a list of homes where they were welcome to stay and I was in two such homes. It was a privilege to have these youngsters attend the meetings and also to witness the great welcome they received from their hosts. What a wonderful idea that was – a great way to bless Israel!

I ended up in the very south of the South Island, again hosted by a family who had never met me. They took me to Bluff, which is like Land's End in Cornwall, truly the very end of the land. I was amazed to find a "finger post" there just as there is at Land's End – a truly wonderful place to pray and make proclamations. We used the Scriptures regarding the Jewish people being called from the "ends of the earth" and such like. It was a powerful time. Even as far south as this there were eight Jewish families who felt safe being so distant (so they thought) from any trouble! No need to go to Israel...

Altogether there were 15 flights and one ten-hour bus journey. The Lord's favour was on me for the flight from Christchurch to Singapore because I was unexpectedly upgraded to business class and treated like a queen. Just imagine, though, when you are about to board and your name is called. I thought that I'd been taken off the very full flight. I was told my seat had been given to someone else and my heart sank. Then came the news that I was upgraded! Not only that but I was assigned my own stewardess who spent most of the journey asking me about Christianity because her sister in Los Angeles had just become a believer. She was eager to find out all about it. So the upgrading had to have been the Lord's doing. What a treat it was too. Hallelujah!

126

11

East Is East and West Is West

I know your deeds. Behold, I have put before you an open door...
(Revelation 3:8)

It was a few months later that the Lord began to impress upon me that I should "go west" and by this He meant to the Caribbean. I was excited. Which islands? I wondered. It soon became clear: Puerto Rico, the Dominican Republic and Cuba. How did this come about? The Lord began to remind me that in 1938, when the nations had gathered in Evian, France, to discuss ways to help the Jews of Nazi Germany, only a few small nations were prepared to do anything. Two of these were the Dominican Republic and Puerto Rico. I knew of nobody in either place and had to check exactly where they were in my atlas, so I had a blank page on which to start. I love it when that is the case because the Lord always fills in the details; we just need to pray and to wait for Him.

It was not long before I knew to add Cuba to the trip. Someone told a Cuban pastor in London that I was going to the Caribbean and he begged me to go to Cuba. His father had just undergone a big operation and needed medical supplies, basic things that were not available there. After prayer, I realized that I should indeed go there so I was even more excited about this trip. I thought there would surely be a number of Jewish people living on each island which would make this a real "fishing trip". I prepared colourful booklets with Scriptures and pictures of Israel to give to the Jewish people that I expected to meet. Maybe God would also open doors in churches for me to share with them about Israel and His Chosen People just as He had done in India, Burma and other places.

I thought it likely that the people would be poor and needy, certainly in Cuba where the Christians were (and still are) persecuted under the Communist regime. I did not know how the Jewish people fared. I packed gifts to take, toiletries, some children's clothing and finances to share as appropriate with Jewish people and the believers. My understanding was that the islands were to some extent primitive with a very hot climate. The Cuban pastor sent a huge package by post. (He had said "just a few small things"!) I was amazed at the contents. Besides all the medical items which included many tablets, a sort of body belt/truss and some bars of soap, there was a round box which contained countless watches, each fastened onto card inside it. Wow, I thought, *I hope the customs officials don't spot these!* I called him to check and he said to be cautious and not to catch the eyes of the customs men. Just walk through! This was for Cuba, but what about the USA and the other places? I was also given two beautiful copies of the Tanach in English and Hebrew as well as seven copies of the New Testament but in Spanish and Hebrew. I wondered who they were for.

~

Going to America, one is allowed extra luggage, which was just as well. I had a large suitcase and a large travel bag, all full. As I prayed, the Lord gave me dates: September 12th to leave and October 3rd to return. The flights out and back were via the USA, then on to San Juan in Puerto Rico for five days before flying on to Santo Domingo in the Dominican Republic. Then I came to a halt. It was not possible to book ongoing flights to Cuba or accommodation there from the UK. It seemed I would have to do it from Santo Domingo. I had no idea how often flights went or to where in Cuba. Whatever happened, I knew I had to be back in Puerto Rico in time for my flight back via the USA. We serve an omnipotent God with whom nothing is impossible. He had set up flights where there were no flights before, as in Chukotka, so I knew I could trust Him.

I was warned about taking items through US customs since I had an overnight stay in Atlanta, Georgia, before going on to Puerto Rico (under US administration). The Lord's Hand proved to be on this trip in a miraculous way because not once on the outward journey were my bags searched at customs – not even opened. It was a different story coming back when I had nothing left to be concerned about! My bags were opened and checked at every place. In Cuba, it was decided that my nail file, which was a part of my nail-clipper, was too long and therefore dangerous, so the man took it! Yet I had been into and out of the US, Puerto Rico and the Dominican Republic without anyone looking at it. That was not all – I was pulled out of the boarding queue and taken back for my big case (now also containing the empty travel bag) to be opened and searched. I was roughly handled, pushed along and rudely spoken to as if I were a criminal, smuggling things! Yet going in, nothing like that happened. No, God had His Mighty Hand over it all.

Puerto Rico

In Puerto Rico I stayed for five days in the capital, San Juan, plus two on the return journey to fit in with flights. It took me two days to find the Jewish people, but then, having made contact, I was invited to visit their Reform synagogue for both Friday evening and Saturday morning services. To my surprise there was a guard at the entrance, checking everyone going in. The people were most welcoming, wanting to hear about Israel, to tell me their own stories about going there, their relatives in the Land and so on. They loved my coloured, pictorial brochures and said that one day maybe they too would go to live there – but not yet. I gave them the two copies of the Tanach, which they were thrilled to receive and announced to everyone as being a great gift.

I asked about anti-Semitism, but it seemed there was none. They did agree that when things got difficult, as I warned them it would one day, they would definitely not delay in going. Some had escaped Hitler and the Nazis, or their families had, so they understood what I was saying.

The next day, Shabbat, they were beginning their celebrations for Rosh Hashanah so I was invited to stay for their Shabbat meal. A rabbi had come for the day, as they did not have their own. He and I had a very interesting conversation about atonement. I showed him a copy of the Hebrew/Spanish New Testament which he very much wanted to have. He said he wanted to read it for himself and asked to keep in touch. Although I did write to him, sadly I did not receive a reply. All I know is these dear Jewish people loved me and I loved them. Puerto Rico has the most Jewish people in all of the islands, about 2,000, and is known as the Commonwealth of the US – very American in style.

All the churches I found, except the Catholic ones, were closed, locked and barred, with no notices or phone numbers. However, the people everywhere were very friendly and wanted to talk to me, thus I had many opportunities to share about the Lord. Most claimed to be Catholics and all were interested to hear about Israel so at least I could speak with some of them individually, if not in a group setting. Maybe, now, after all these years, some of the Jewish people have gone to Israel, I do not know.

The Dominican Republic

The next place the Lord directed me to was Santo Domingo in the Dominican Republic. Here I had a beautiful hotel, centrally placed, for four nights. There were few guests so I was made very welcome indeed! After constant enquiries I learned that there was definitely one synagogue and it was thought to be in a certain area – only no one was certain! The phone book and yellow pages were of no help to get either a phone number or an address. First though, I needed to book a return flight to Cuba which was only possible from here. I set off on foot to find the office and prayed about the dates. I thought the Lord was saying the 22nd to 29th, which would give me a whole week there. As always He is right. Those were the very dates on which the plane flew! It did not go every day as I had expected but only once a week. Thankfully I was able to book seats for flights to the capital, Havana.

Having done that, I set out on foot again to the area where the synagogue might be located. It was very hot – 36 degrees Celsius – and a very long way. Every street I tried proved useless and I became extremely tired and thirsty. I prayed for somewhere to buy a drink, somewhere shady, a place to rest. Very soon I saw a shop with seats under some awnings where young people were drinking coke. They were aiming their empty cans unsuccessfully at a waste bin. The university was nearby so I guessed they were students.

Thankfully I found a corner for a rest with an ice-cold drink. Then suddenly, three very pretty girls stood in front of me. Was I lost? Did I need help? We had a lovely conversation – they were all law students – and as to the synagogue, why it was just around the corner – they could take me there! If that was not the Lord's help, then whose was it?

Soon we were there and the girls went cheerfully on their way. I stood outside two large white gates at least 8 feet tall, bearing a large black-painted Star of David on each. They were locked. No one answered the bell and there was no sign of life through the gap in the gates. There were no notices either, nothing that revealed any activity at all. What should I do now? I walked on and on, later finding a place in which to have a snack. I checked the map I had, and the easiest route back (though still a long way) was through t he campus of the university. I had a strong impression that I would meet a Jewish man as I walked that way, so I started praying to find him.

The route back was indeed a long way but it was attractive with flower gardens and blossoming trees. I was watching the people, all the while praying expectantly for this person. Once through the campus, I reached a small roundabout with a rose garden in the centre. As I walked around the left-hand side. there he was – a most Jewish-looking man. He looked at me and I looked at him. He seemed to know.

"Well, hello," he said, as if he knew me.

I smiled back. "You are Jewish?" I asked him.

He agreed, "Of course", and so we talked and talked, it seemed for ages. He told me there were very few Jewish people in Santo Domingo; more lived in a town much further north. There were so few that the synagogue was only opened twice a month and there wasn't really any sort of community activity. I showed him the aliyah brochures, which he gladly took and expressed an interest in their contents. Before leaving the hotel that morning, I'd had a strong impression to take a copy of the Hebrew/Spanish New Testament with me. I still had it in my bag when the Holy Spirit began to nudge me to offer it to him. I don't usually do this sort of thing but the nudge was strong. As I hesitantly took it out of my bag, he spotted it and with great joy asked "Oh, where did you get that? It is just what I want for my studies. We cannot get them here. I can share it with my friends for our essays." Well, I was amazed, speechless. The Lord always knows best and I had nearly disobeyed Him.

He said he would be in touch with me at my hotel, as he wanted to meet me again. But he did not do so, maybe because the telephone was often not working.

The next day, I went to the Israeli Embassy in a taxi chauffeured by a helpful driver called Lara. It was too far to walk and the sun was even hotter than yesterday! The embassy was heavily guarded and I was not allowed in. The guard, who was in a secure pillbox, spoke by mobile to a young man who came outside. He was an

Israeli from Tel Aviv who confirmed what the other man had told me. He too accepted brochures for aliyah and agreed to pass them on. As he went back inside, two others appeared and, along with the security guard, chatted to me about the lack of Jewish activity in the town. I felt a strong nudge on my arm and so brought out of my bag three of the Spanish/Hebrew New Testaments and offered them to these lads. They each took one when they saw the Hebrew. To my surprise they wanted them, receiving them gladly and smiling. And that was that. As I returned to the hotel in the taxi, I felt strange – no churches open, the synagogue closed and just individuals to talk to. It was strange and I felt bereft. Only God knew what He was doing.

~

Back at the hotel, I confided to the man at the desk that I had to find a hotel in Cuba. Having accommodation booked was one of the requirements for entry but impossible to set up. He was most helpful, telling me he was himself from Cuba but had "escaped". He knew the names of hotels in Havana where I was headed and said he would help me to call them. Maybe I could book that way. He listed some names and the telephone operator tried to put us through to Cuba, to connect with one of them. It proved to be impossible. The operator apologized; he was a really kind man. They all were, in fact. I don't think they had many visitors from England! Even in the restaurant, the waiters and waitresses would gather round me to ask me about myself and life in England. When I left, they were all hugging me goodbye!

Cuba

Cuba was a different story. Here I had to get my luggage myself and also had no hotel booked, a requirement on the entry form. I can only say, again, that when God says, "I have gone before you and prepared the way", He has everything planned. So we should not be surprised when we find He has done just that. The man in the hotel in Santo Domingo had given me a list of good hotels so I just put the first one on the form, hoping it would be the one. I did not want to be untruthful.

At the airport, a man returning to Cuba began to chat to me, and when we arrived in Havana, he walked through with me, helping me to get my luggage, showing me the way. I am sure it was because he walked with me that we just went through, no questions asked, nothing. With the hold-all of stuff the Cuban pastor in England had given me – medical supplies, including lots of pills, and all those watches – I could have been in trouble had they searched me, but I just walked through! Suddenly I was outside. The man went off somewhere and I did not see him again to thank him. Near the exit to the road was a place where you could book a hotel. I prayed the Lord would give me His choice and was sent to one which the lady thought would suit me. Well, it did, and had to be the Lord's choice because it proved to be small and only ten minutes' walk from the nearest synagogue one way and ten minutes' walk from a big charismatic Methodist church another way. In fact I was near to everything I needed! The lady ordered me a taxi and soon I was made very welcome and safely installed in a comfortable room.

~

Having endured a Communist regime (at that time for 45 years) fashioned on Russian ways, the first thing apparent in Cuba was the poverty. The houses, unrepaired in all this time, were in a terrible state of decay, with broken windows, old Spanish-type balconies and crumbling pillars, rusted railings and doors falling off. It needed to be seen to be believed. It was worse than East Germany was after 25 years.

A few roads were OK, but most were full of potholes. People grumble about the roads in the UK, but you should have seen these.

People who did have cars played dodgem, zigzagging along to avoid the worst holes. Then the cars – you'd have thought they came from a museum. There were old American styles with the fluted backs, plus some European vintage Ladas and Skodas – all emitting black smoke... ugh. The buses were the same, including one called a "camel" bus. It had two parts joined by a lower section which swivelled. Needless to say, they were always packed and steaming in the heat – with smoking allowed too. I only tried one. That was more than enough!

After enquiring, I was told there was a synagogue nearby so I set off to find it. To my surprise, the doors were wide open and I could just walk in. There was no security here. I was made very welcome and told there were no problems and no restrictions on being Jewish, not like there were for Christians. There was no anti- Semitism but, of course, Jews could not leave the country, even if they wanted to. I was shown around, taken down to see their library and invited to come to their services, both on Friday evening and again on Saturday morning when they would also have lunch. They had a store for medicines and clothing for the poor, too. I told them I had some things to share and arranged to bring them another time.

Later that day I set off to find the Methodist church – a huge substantial building – and also a Pentecostal church a little further on. I learned that things for them were a little easier in that they could go to church but that was all. No meetings outside the church were allowed, certainly no house groups. In fact all the house churches had been closed. I also learned that things were not easier for Christians in rural areas where there was still much persecution. Many were in prison. Some had been locked away for 20–25 years and badly treated. I know that even today this situation remains true. To get on, you had to be a Communist; otherwise it could be difficult to get a good job, just as it was in the fSU for both Jews and Christians. It was good though – and quite unusual – that the Jewish people were not ostracized.

In the churches, I was invited to share with the leaders but not with the congregations; that was not allowed. I was able to convey to the leaders, with interpreters, the message about God's plans and purposes for Israel according to the Scriptures and how we need to pray. They loved it and said this was vital teaching, and that all the churches needed to hear this message. They wanted it written out, so I made three copies as a Bible study, giving all the scriptural references; six pages each in all. It took time doing it by hand, but was worth the effort. They could get it translated and use it to pass on to other churches. I did three because a lady came to visit me in the hotel. She was from an Assemblies of God (AOG) church and eager to hear the message, and so three denominations received the teaching.

Then there was all the aid which I had brought. I had to take a taxi to find the family of the Cuban pastor in London. It was a very long way out of town and so I saw much of the poverty of the island – people living in run-down shacks and working in the fields doing things by hand. They were all cheerful, nevertheless. The taxi man helped me to find the run-down bungalow where the family lived and he insisted on staying to take me back, for which I was grateful. They knew little English and were obviously very poor, with hardly any furniture and just a lot of old clothes lying around. The place needed a lot of repair with some of the ceiling having fallen in and windows missing. They were very grateful when I handed over the bag from their son but did not give more than a cursory glance inside. I was glad of that as the taxi man might have spotted the watches! It was incredibly hot, yet they did not offer me a drink, probably because they could not afford it. Or maybe their cups were too cracked to offer a guest? Who knows? They were all Christians and hugged me as I left. I was very glad I had taken them the help and also gave them some soap and a little finance from what I had.

The rest of the aid I divided into three sets, which meant two large carrier bags each for the synagogue and each for the two churches. At that time I did not know about the lady from AOG.

However, I still had some soap, shampoo and finance that I could give her as the Lord had shown me to save some. He always knows everything! I had changed £100 into local money for each of the three, which they could use to help the really poor. I had learned from talking to them that they each provided simple meals to the elderly, widows and widowers and single mothers with children, to keep them from starving. What a life it was out there. I heard that often the children had to go to school having eaten nothing.

There were two forms of money in Cuba. The tourists had convertible pesos, one peso being equal to a bit less than a dollar. The people had national pesos. They needed 25 of these to get one of the type I had! Thus their money was really worthless. They could not shop where tourists bought things – as in the fSU and North Korea. They had their own shops, which were virtually empty. I saw long queues for bread with a man with a truncheon controlling the number entering to buy, so the queue only moved on slowly. Most people earned about 200–250 pesos monthly, an inadequate amount unless more than one in the household had a job.

First I took the two bags to the synagogue where they were overjoyed to receive the gifts and finances. The medicines were stored away in a special cupboard and administered by a doctor, although really they were only basic items like aspirin, antiseptic creams, plasters etc. – all unobtainable there. I wished I could have taken more. They loved the clothing, especially the baby items. It was the same with the churches. My heart ached when I saw the need, and I returned very tearful to my hotel.

At the synagogue I was invited to stay for lunch and made to feel like one of the family. They all longed to go to Israel and assured me that whenever it became possible they would definitely go. I do not know to this day if they have been allowed out. I still had three of the Hebrew/Spanish New Testaments and I wondered what to do with them, hesitating to say anything. I did not want to offend them in any way. However, the Lord always has a plan. The lady in the library was chatting to me and showed me the books they had – all old now and much read. We began to talk about the Bible and again I felt a nudge to show her the New Testaments – I had three left. When she saw the Hebrew she agreed to have one for her library. I was surprised at this and gave it to her. Then one of the ladies from the synagogue who was from Argentina came along. When she saw the New Testaments, she took the other two. It was all so surprising. I wasn't trying to convert anyone, just obeying the leading of the Lord.

What a journey it proved to be; so different from going east, so many contacts and opportunities. I came back praising God all the way for the churches in Cuba, eager to learn about Israel and God's purposes. And the Jewish people eager to make aliyah as soon as they could. What more could I have asked for? Maybe today they can go. Maybe too they are going from the Dominican Republic and from Puerto Rico, since today there is an aliyah move among the Spanish-speaking (Sephardic) Jewish people. I hope I meet some!

12

Back to the East – China

I will take you one from a city and two from a family, And I will bring you to Zion.

(Jeremiah 3:14)

"Esther, have you ever heard of the Kaifeng Jews?" So enquired a friend who frequently went to China. She told me how, through someone else, she had located and visited them. A great excitement filled my heart as I realized this would be my next adventure. Ripple, as she was called, insisted on setting up the journey, for which I was very glad since she had been to China 38 times. She knew exactly how to go about it all and had contacts there, whereas I had none. We agreed that we would make it a joint trip as she needed to revisit some children's homes and a mysterious person she called her "secret agent". Then we would go to find the Jewish people. I couldn't wait!

People are wonderful, for in response to a newsletter, I received an abundant supply of warm hats, scarves, gloves and socks which I was able to take for the children in the homes we visited. They were so excited and loved trying them on and choosing what they wanted. We also took vitamins and other supplies, including some DVDs which they had asked for. We had seven large bags or cases full when we met at London Heathrow. Of these seven, three were mine so you can imagine how much was sent to me.

When we set off, there were three of us – Ripple, me, plus a man called Les who had often travelled with Ripple. He was almost 100% deaf which caused some amusing incidents! For example, he would misunderstand where we were meeting and had to be found, or did not hear his alarm or our hammering on his door to wake him up. In addition to this, Ripple had Hodgkin's disease (cancer of the lymph glands), which was in an advanced stage. Four years before, she had been given two months to live! She did not let this stop her from doing the Lord's work, however, and continued with her ministry regardless, just using a wheelchair wherever there was a lot of walking in the airports. She had pre-arranged all this and was amazing in her persistence.

Leijian

We entered China from Hong Kong where we obtained our visas and air tickets for travel within the country. Here, too, Ripple knew exactly where to go and even knew the people in the office! Once supplied, we set off for the border, with Ripple in a wheelchair as we walked a long way beneath a wide tunnel trundling all the luggage. In the centre, we had to exchange the wheelchair for a Chinese one before continuing. We stayed overnight just inside China and the next day flew to a pretty little town called Leijian, to the far west, in the Himalayan foothills. We spent a few days visiting four children's homes set up as families with 10–12 children in each. Their ages ranged from about 8 to 17 or 18. This was part of an experiment, an idea of a Finnish lady, observed as a pattern for the future by the Chinese authorities, but funded by Western missions. The children obviously all knew Ripple and called her "Grandma" – a title they gave to me as well. We had meals with them – just like being in a large family; it was great fun. There was always someone to translate into English and the children made us laugh trying to say the words.

On Sunday morning we were invited to a time of fellowship – in fact a secret church meeting. We were taken into a courtyard and up some stairs to a landing where a young man was apparently using a computer. He was in fact watching who came and went. Inside was a long room where a number of people were sitting on sofas and armchairs enjoying tea, coffee and biscuits. It looked just like a friendly "coffee morning". People arrived in ones or twos in order not to attract attention – just as they did in the fSU. We were greatly welcomed. After some gentle soft singing, they all listened to an audio-tape message which was in Mandarin. It was such a privilege to be there with them.

The Chinese secret police (PSB) constantly came round checking up. There were churches existing (and are still) but they had to be registered and to obey rules about what they taught. It was not free in any way. Hence in China there were hundreds of house churches which were not registered. Christians were much persecuted and the leaders regularly taken in and beaten up, imprisoned on false charges or even executed. This continues to happen today. Many of you will have read the book *The Heavenly Man* by Brother Yun, which tells of the real situation. If you have not done so, do please read it – an awesome story of God's Hand on the life of the author.

In the evenings we went into the old town centre, which had been restored in traditional style and was very pretty. The little houses had typical turned-up Chinese-style roofs. There was a little river flowing through the centre, colourful lanterns lighting the way, and dozens of pretty little shops along the narrow cobbled streets. We did much of our Christmas shopping there. It seemed that Ripple had many friends who welcomed us into their shops, sold us things or served us hot chocolate. It was truly a special time. The town had been restored as a Heritage Site and attracted many tourists.

Xian

After a few days in Leijian, we flew on to the next place – a big city in the centre of the country – called Xian, known for the discovery of the Terracotta Soldiers. These are life-size pottery models of the army of a Chinese emperor, who long ago had expected to be raised from the dead along with his army. When he died, all his soldiers were buried with him – alive or dead, I do not know. A horrible story nevertheless.

The city was said to be flourishing due to the growth of the Chinese economy and that is what it seemed like. There were Chinese people who were getting rich, and left behind were the very poor. Our contact was Ripple's "secret agent" who ran a pizza restaurant with some sweet-faced Chinese girls, all believers. It was a cover for whatever else she did and that was very special. This work had started when she noticed starving children hanging around the shop. They ran away when she went outside. However, she followed them and discovered dozens of hungry people living rough under a huge bridge. Their needs were great. Lost and abandoned, sick, injured, mentally or physically disabled, they were out on the street. It seemed that all medical treatment had to be paid for, but as these folk could not work, they had no money to pay for their needs. There was no social security here, no National Health Service – nothing.

Ripple's friend – let's call her Sue – had set to work to raise money for these people, hence the shop. In addition, supporters from UK sent donations to her (I do not know how), and with this finance she took hope to these abandoned people. She provided warm food, blankets, medical help in the form of visits to doctors or hospitals for operations – whatever was needed. There were men with frost- bite and gangrenous feet, some with broken limbs, some so sick they could not clean themselves. There was so much pain and suffering there. Just to wash a face, to show you cared, would cause them to weep and weep. We met these people and saw their suffering for ourselves.

Sue held quiet meetings whenever possible in a small shed nearby in order to tell them about the Lord who loves them – it was a really special work going on. Naturally, she had to be careful that the Chinese secret police did not find out. They rarely entered the place under the bridge as no one was supposed to know about the situation of the really poor. In China there was no provision for the poor. We in the West have no idea… Praise God we were able to add to Sue's finances from gifts given to us.

It was while we were in this city that Ripple often mentioned that her leg ached, but she brushed it aside saying it was nothing unusual. I noticed she did sit down as often as possible – but go to a doctor? Never!

Kaifeng

The next trip we had to make was a long all-day train ride to my real destination and the reason I had gone to China – to Kaifeng, where there is no airport. Here still live a community who claim to be of the Chosen People. I say it that way because there has been much intermarriage over the past 100–200 years. The story goes that 900 years ago, seven Jewish traders travelled along the Silk Road and, with permission from the emperor, settled in this city. The emperor gave them Chinese names which all the families still use today: Mr Jeng, Mr Jung, Mr Heng and so on.

They stayed there with their families, having their own worship centre and keeping to their faith. However, as years passed, trading declined and they became very poor. Their synagogue was washed away in a flood in 1850 but they had no money to rebuild another. There is a factory today on the site but a plaque does say that it was there. With no rabbi to guide them, they gradually they lost their special ways and became more or less assimilated, still retaining their Chinese family names. I couldn't wait to meet them.

A young American lad, called Tim, met us from the train and took us to our hotel. It seemed he had gone to Kaifeng to find the Jewish people and was helping them to rediscover their Jewishness and to learn some Hebrew. Meantime he was trying to find a way for them to go to Israel where his own family lived. To my surprise, he recognized me – remembering meeting me at his Israeli home, then in Tiberias, when he was only 13! I had gone there on behalf of Christian Friends of Israel (CFI), as his mother was distributing clothes to the new olim, and we wanted to pass on some to help her. What a small world it is – and I was amazed he remembered me! It was he who had told Ripple about this Jewish community and so here we were!

The next day, Tim took us to the Jewish area. The houses were very small, all joined together, and the streets very narrow with tiny shops where people were selling clothes. Wonderfully, the main street was called "The Street of the Reading of the Torah"! We met several of the people, but hardly anyone knew any English. They wanted us to go into their tiny homes, which were dark and barely furnished, to share coffee and little Chinese savouries – a sort of biscuit or cake. They were so friendly and excited that we had come. One or two tried out their Hebrew, but just imagine it with a Chinese accent – unrecognizable to me!

We visited one old lady, apparently in her late eighties, though she was unsure of her exact birth date. She lived alone in one room, in very primitive conditions, where she kept a few very old Jewish items – a menorah, candlesticks and two crowns which would cap the Torah Scrolls. In addition she had a few other items, unidentifiable to me but which she proudly showed us. She had the sweetest smiling face, so serene and peaceful. It was obvious the others looked after her as there was no water or other facilities in her room.

Many of these people had records of their family line and knew who they were. There were about 600 of them altogether and they all wanted to go to Israel. In 1996, the Chinese authorities collected their identity cards and then reissued them with Chinese registration. This meant that they had no documents identifying them as being Jewish. In one place they had old photos of family groups with people dressed in Jewish-style religious garments and they would point out relatives, but of course this did not prove anything acceptable for the Jewish Agency.

Tim had arranged through the Israeli Embassy in Beijing for

a group of youngsters aged 16+ to go to Israel as tourists. The intention was that they would stay there to study Hebrew and do a conversion course. Then they could make aliyah. They would have to do the conversion course as they had no way to prove their Jewishness. He brought four of these teenagers forward to meet us. Their parents were bravely letting them go, which was really something as they would not see them again for a long time, if ever. Years later, when in Israel, I met one of the girls again; she had married one of the boys, so obviously they had succeeded in their effort to live in Israel. That was wonderful. She also told me of others who had come to Israel too.

On Shabbat we had a special meal and many of the Jewish people gathered there with us. This was in Tim's flat. In the garden he had a *succah* (booth) as they had recently celebrated the Feast of Tabernacles – all a part of Tim's teaching. It happened to be my birthday on that day, but no one knew. As they sang some Jewish songs and enjoyed the food, I sat there wondering at the mighty Hand of God who had set this up. Here I was in China, sharing a meal with these virtually unknown Jewish people. It seemed quite incredible. We stayed there for three days.

The greatest need of these people was for finance, both for travel and to use in Israel. Many people had sent me gifts amounting to £600 which I was able to give to Tim to use in helping these very poor people, some of whom went to Israel eventually.

~

It was during these last days that Ripple became very poorly. She had a problem with a very painful leg and also with her breathing, so much so that for the last two nights we were there she could not sleep and I sat up with her to help. Les had been a nurse and, looking at her swollen leg, he was convinced she had a DVT (deep vein thrombosis). She told us that on the flight out from the UK to Hong Kong, she had slept for the whole journey. Even though we had been sitting together, we had not noticed. We realized now that she should have walked about at least once every two hours. Despite her condition, Ripple would not have a doctor. She was advised to keep her leg up but this was hard for her as she could not breathe without sitting on the side of the bed. What was strange, however, was that when visitors arrived (some of the Jewish folk came to see her), she would brighten up and seem much better. On our last night a whole family of Jewish people came to say "goodbye", together with a little girl. She sat up on the bed with Ripple who seemed quite well, laughing and happy. We truly thought she was somehow miraculously better. However, once they had gone, we had another sleepless night when she was in much pain and hardly able to breathe.

Our return journey was to have been by bus to another town, and then a ferry to Hong Kong. It was a long route that would have saved money, but it was not to be as we realized that Ripple would not manage all the changes. Instead Tim and Les booked a direct flight to Hong Kong where she could rest for a day before our long flight to the UK. Early on our last morning, while I packed both our cases, the men brought a wheelchair and took Ripple to a bus that they had booked to take us to the airport. After checking in we said our farewells and one of the staff took us through to board the aircraft. Two stewardesses took charge of Ripple to help her up the steps into the cabin while I followed behind. Our booked seats were near the back of the plane but the cabin crew decided to put Ripple in an aisle seat near the front on the fourth row. They asked me what was wrong so I told them she was very tired, which was true since she had not slept all night. I sat across the aisle, hoping it was not someone else's seat.

Ripple asked for a drink of water and then wanted something to eat. She sipped most of the water but needed me to hold the beaker and also support her head as she seemed unable to do so herself. She also tried to eat a small apricot but without success. I signalled for Les to come and sit with us as the front of the plane was almost empty. As the stewardess came round with drinks, Ripple wanted some tea. I put half into a beaker and helped her to drink it. Her head kept falling forward and I asked her to lift it. "I can't," she said, in an almost inaudible voice. Eventually she did and I asked her if she would like more tea. When I turned back with the second half-beaker, her head had flopped forward again. As I lifted her head to give her the tea, I suddenly realized she had died! Her lips were purple and her eyes fixed. There was no doubt about it – she had passed away, just like that, in a few seconds!

Quietly came the gentle voice of the Lord: "*Don't tell the crew. Lay her down, put her head on a pillow and a blanket over her. She is asleep.*" I followed the instructions exactly and then told Les what had happened. Since he was so deaf it took a while for him to understand my whispering! He was sure she was just unconscious so went to check her pulse. He could find none and agreed she was no longer alive. We continued the flight until we reached Hong Kong. The stewardesses went through the plane to check that all seats were upright – the usual procedure – but did not even notice that Ripple was lying down!

As she had been brought to the plane in a wheelchair we had to wait until everyone else was off the plane before we could get off. This is when I did my Oscar performance. I went as if to wake Ripple, and then went to tell a crew member that I could not wake her. Of course they also checked and then came and said they thought she had died. I immediately burst into tears and was comforted by the stewardess, though strangely, I had not cried earlier, when she had actually died.

First the Chinese medics had to come to confirm the death, then the Chinese police. This all took a long time. Next the Hong Kong doctors and police came to check. They asked if they should send her to the hospital or to the mortuary. We said the mortuary, which made more sense since they had pronounced her dead. They wanted to issue a death certificate but we did not have enough Hong Kong money. Meanwhile the cleaners were waiting to come on board. We were not popular. In the end a van was driven to the aircraft and Ripple's body was taken away, and Les and I were escorted to the airport police station for questioning in case we had done the deed!

A Hong Kong policeman with two guns in his belt sat across from us at a desk. He called us "Mr and Mrs Lever" so I corrected him saying, "He is not my husband, just a friend", to which he replied, "It's all right. We understand"! He directed his questions at me instead of Les, so probably someone had told him Les was deaf. It took a long time as he asked all about my background, family and why we were in China, laboriously writing down everything in English. Then it had to be translated into Chinese which also took ages. We became extremely hungry so I asked if we could get a drink and something to eat. Nearby was a policewoman shouting at everyone and being very bossy but she became very friendly towards us, ordering sandwiches and juice straight away and without charging us at all.

In the meantime the policeman had gone away to ensure the translation was done. On his return he told us that we would have to go to the mortuary the next morning to identify the body. Well, we had no idea where it was and Hong Kong is a huge city. I asked him if we could be picked up and taken there. After phoning someone, he agreed – we'd be picked up at 8.00 a.m. Then thankfully we were allowed to go. We took a taxi to a flat where we'd been offered accommodation and the first thing I did was phone Ripple's husband to tell him the news. Although stunned, he took it very well and set about arranging to bring her body back to the UK. After a much- needed good night's sleep, I managed to wake Les in the next room to be ready to go to the mortuary. We went down into the street to wait. Unbelievably, our transport to the mortuary was a prison van complete with barred windows! I have travelled in many unusual vehicles but this was the biggest laugh yet. The policeman from the day before, complete with high boots and guns, led us like two criminals into the van as pedestrians watched us suspiciously. Then we were securely locked in and driven away!

The mortuary was not yet open and we had to wait in a queue for our turn. We were first interviewed by a man in a green robe. He also called us "Mr and Mrs Lever", which drew the same response when I said Les was not Mr Lever! This man went through lots of questions about how Ripple had died before we were allowed to identify her body. Then we were led out of another door for another time of questioning and a decision from us as to whether there should be a post-mortem. We thought not, although they actually did perform one to see whether or not she had died of Asian flu, swine fever or TB. It was three weeks before the body was brought to England.

From the mortuary, we were told we must go to see a lawyer on behalf of Ripple's husband who was making arrangements from England for the return of her body and belongings. Here we had another adventure, for we took a taxi there – another long journey through the city to a huge building surrounded by many large white buses. The taxi driver had to drop us within walking distance, so we weaved our way through many people, all in white, carrying huge bouquets of white flowers. "Must be a wedding," mused Les. But then we realized it was a funeral, Buddhist style. All the people were going to the same building as we were.

Eventually we managed to get inside and were directed to the eighth floor where we found a Mr Chung awaiting us. We could not miss the Buddha idol on a side shelf, complete with candle and food. All this was new to me. It still amazes me that an educated lawyer could put food in front of a statue. However, he was most helpful to us. I had to assume Power of Attorney for Ripple's husband, David, and then sign for various things, including her passport, rings and a few other things, and for her body to be sent to England – unless she was found to have died from one of the three diseases. In that case she would be buried locally in Hong Kong. What a business it was.

As for Ripple, she finished the course, completed the race. She saw all the work in which she had been involved in her beloved

China, and the Lord had taken her while she was still out there. Later on I heard from her husband, David, that on his retirement he had set money aside each month for Ripple and the last payment had been that month. Also her mobile-phone contract had finished that month. Amazing! It seemed everything had been arranged so neatly and tidily. What a great God we serve. The large church where Ripple's memorial service was held was filled to capacity as so many people knew her. Some of them shared amazing testimonies from her life. I count it a privilege that I was with her on her last journey and that she led me to find the Jews of Kaifeng. Today their situation is being examined by the authorities, so perhaps they will be allowed to make aliyah one day after all. I pray it happens

13

The First Unusual Tour Group –
Syria

*I will gather you from the peoples and assemble you out of the
countries among which you have been scattered, and I will give
you the land of Israel.*

(Ezekiel 11:17)

"Esther, I want you to go to countries that are not friendly towards
Israel, from where My people are not allowed to make aliyah." This
caused me to protest as I could not see the point in going. Then the
Lord reminded me of times I had helped Jewish people to go to
Israel when their situations had been impossible – from Leningrad
and from Riga, in Latvia. Both times, the Lord had made a way. I
repented. Where, I wondered, would God want me to go this time?
The answer came – Syria!

Shortly after that, at New Year in 2007, I was reading a newsletter
from someone who had gone to Syria and also Lebanon. Immediately
my spirit was alerted so I contacted the writer. He encouraged me to
go, but warned I should go with a tour group as otherwise it would
not be safe. He said there were Christians, mainly Orthodox, who
were basically all OK, and a few Jewish people, with whom and for
whom it would be dangerous to be seen talking as a Westerner. In
other words I needed to be very careful. The only tour group going
into Syria was "Voyages Jules Verne" – very expensive! However, it

did give five optional extra days in which to explore the delights of Damascus. I had a strong prompting to include these extra days.

I met a Christian from Syria who told me that if I went as a private tourist, I would be closely questioned and watched. This was confirmed by another lady whose husband had gone to Syria on business. Not only was he watched, but all his belongings in the hotel had been thoroughly searched! This convinced me to book with "Jules Verne". Where God guides, He provides and so He did – abundantly.

By the time the trip was set up, it was June. There were others joining the tour from the UK and then we all met up in Damascus, enough people to fill a coach, and from several countries, but they all spoke English. They were people who love to travel, so much of their talk was of where they had been – cruises, unusual destinations and so on, all flavoured with one-upmanship. And of course they questioned me as well about the motives for my journey. I told them I was a Christian, which they did not seem to mind, and that my travelling was mostly for humanitarian aid purposes, after which they more or less left me alone. There were a few opportunities to talk about the Lord so I prayed He would water the seed. Nothing is wasted with Him!

Each day we travelled out to visit archaeological sites: Roman, Byzantine and from the Crusader period, which proved to be very strenuous. We visited citadels, castles and old churches. Many were way out in the desert where the temperature was 44 degrees Celsius or more, while others were in ancient cities, high up in the hills, involving climbing up steps or over rocky areas – very dusty and difficult. The temperature everywhere was always somewhere between 32 and 40 °C.

One place has recently been in the news – Palmyra – the site of an ancient Roman city. (At the time of writing, it has been taken by ISIS – the so-called Islamic State in Iraq and Syria – and partially destroyed.) We walked through it from one end to the other and back! It was here that I realized most of the group were "Roman-remains fanatics"! I wasn't. However, it was a time for prayer, prophetic actions and proclamations done quietly without the others noticing. And I did get a free ride on a camel – great fun but a bit scary as the lad made the animal run!

We stopped in Aleppo for about an hour and walked through the typically Arab market. I understood that a few Jewish people lived there and thought that some might have a market stall, but it was impossible to tell. In any case there was little time to make contact. Today much of Aleppo has been destroyed in the recent war, so who knows if any Jews remain there.

As a part of the tour, we spent two days in Lebanon. This did not give me time to find the Jewish people, except for some teenage girls drinking juice at a café in Beirut where we stopped. They were Jewish – each wearing a Star of David necklace – and told me their families worked there. From the bus the guide showed me the old synagogue, and told me that 500 Jewish people still lived in Lebanon. *Why?* I asked myself, when the border to Israel was so near. *Why do they stay here?* The country was peaceful at that time and much like northern Israel – beautiful and very clean. I longed to go again to find some of those remaining 500! Our guide was a Christian Arab who confided so to me, saying she was really called Maya, but uses "Maha" as it was safer for her among the Muslims.

~

Back in Damascus, I now had five days, which included two day-excursions. I felt clearly led to participate in them. What a blessing this proved to be – the highlight of the trip. On day one, we arrived back and had just the afternoon free. I spent time weeping before the Lord because I could see no way of connecting with Jewish people. With only four days left, what could I do?

Day two was one of the trips out. Syria was where Paul established some of today's oldest churches – now very orthodox and religious. (Under the recent attacks of ISIS, many of the believers have been killed or driven away and the churches destroyed.) To my surprise, we were taken to visit two of these very ancient churches, built into the sides of the rocky hills. The place was Ma-aloula where the people still spoke Aramaic. We had a new guide that day, Abdullah, an Orthodox Christian who came from this village. It was a beautiful place, sadly now destroyed in today's fighting. Apparently all the Christians have been driven out.

On the way back, as we approached our hotel, I had a distinct impression I should ask Abdullah if there were any Jewish people left in Syria. I had been told that Jews had been allowed to go to New York in 1992, but not to Israel, and also that all synagogues had been destroyed. I waited until we were in the vestibule. He told me that there were about five families in Aleppo and maybe 50–100 Jewish people in Damascus. Then he looked me straight in the eye before taking out a piece of paper and drawing me a little map to show me where to go in the Old City of Damascus. He told me that a Jewish man had a shop there, "and his name is George," he said. What a wonderful God we serve. No wonder I had to go on that tour!

I set off the next morning, finding my way through some narrow cobbled streets, following Abdullah's simple map. Rounding a bend, I saw the shop at the next corner. It was quite large, selling antiques, carpets, silks, jewellery and such like. The owners were obviously quite wealthy. There were two men inside who welcomed me, obviously thinking I was a rich Western customer. I explained that I had come to see George, only to be told he was not there – he had gone abroad. His son John was due any minute so I said I would wait for him. I was politely offered a chair and cup of Arab coffee while they phoned to check. It seemed he would be an hour. I still said I would wait. In the meantime I talked to the men, whose names were Salim and Claude. John did not appear so I went to explore the building next door, a former palace and now a museum with a garden. Here I could pray.

On my return, another man was in the shop, inside a sort of

raised semicircular desk. "Oh, are you John?" I asked, to which he replied that he was Albert and that John was not coming after all. Curious about their names, I asked Albert why, if they were Jewish, they had Christian Arab names. He explained that it was safer for them. This was curious as people obviously knew they were Jews. I talked with Albert and told him the Lord's message – that He had not forgotten them. Also that they should go to Israel, quoting some Scriptures relating to the ingathering. Albert said that if they went to the "other place" (he would not dare say the name), he would never be able to come back to Syria, to their business. Their families were in New York and they could go there to visit. He implied that things were safe for them there, that there were no problems. After we had finished our conversation Albert arranged for Claude to take me to the synagogue on Friday where I might meet a few more Jewish people. I was delighted.

Leaving the shop, I went exploring what was apparently the old Jewish Quarter – Albert's shop was on the very edge. Mostly deserted, it consisted of semi-derelict homes behind padlocked iron doors in narrow streets and alleyways; an old ghetto area to be sure. A few Jewish people still lived there among some Arab families who had moved in. I saw one lady, who looked very Jewish, buying vegetables outside a tiny shop. She answered me in French when I spoke to her, but her face broke into a smile when I asked her quietly if she were Jewish. She held my hands briefly, realized we were being watched and immediately withdrew, disappearing into a very narrow alleyway. She was very afraid. *Why, why are they still here?* I asked myself. It was certainly not safe, even if Albert said it was.

Walking on, I found myself in the Christian Quarter on a narrow winding road with a famous name – it was labelled "A Street called Straight". Wow, I thought! Soon I came across the house of Ananias, with a church built over it – of course! I felt I was back in the Book of Acts. Another road, also very narrow, was called Bar Touma or Thomas Street where there was a tiny Christian bookshop. The young lady inside assured me that things were quiet for them, and people were fairly free to be believers in Jesus in Damascus. At that point two sweet-faced women came in. They told me they were from northern Iraq. They had fled to Syria with their children along with hundreds of others, because their churches were being destroyed and people murdered. This was in 2006. Today, ISIS is finishing off the churches and because of its violence there are millions of refugees. My heart aches for these dear believers. Where are they now? Are they alive, or have they all been killed?

A little further on was the old city wall in which was a tiny window high up – reputedly where Paul was let down to escape his persecutors! It was quite an adventure.

~

Friday came and off I went to meet Claude who was waiting for me in a shiny bright Mercedes – belonging to George, he told me. He drove me way out into a much poorer area of Damascus, into a narrow street where we parked the car next to a high wall. On the wall was an unreadable dusty plaque beside two iron gates. Claude hammered on them with his fist and shouted to someone who came and opened one door. Inside was what looked like a builder's yard. However, hidden to the right was the synagogue with ornate doors decorated with Jewish symbols. Claude rang a bell which was answered by a sweet-faced man who did not want to tell me his name. He did not speak either English or French so Claude told him why I had come and he welcomed me inside.

It was the most beautiful synagogue, with wonderful chandeliers and rich carpets. It was called the Jobar Synagogue, the oldest in Europe, dating from about 1200. It seemed that it was not used much, mainly on feast days. The dear man opened the Ark of the Covenant for me, took out one of the ancient Torah Scrolls and allowed me to read a little. What a privilege. Then he took us to a special little corner sectioned off like a small chapel. We took off our shoes and went through a door, inside which was a narrow staircase winding down to a tiny room about 1.5 square metres. It had little arched niches with small candles in them, but it all felt so holy, so precious, and there was such a presence of the Lord. I thought they were telling me that the prophet Elijah was buried here – or did they mean he had visited or prayed there? I wasn't sure.

We lit two candles and as I began the prayer in Hebrew for lighting the Sabbath candles, the men joined in joyfully. Then we said the Shema together and finally sang it right through. I cannot put into words the wonderful, precious atmosphere that pervaded that tiny room. The Lord was in it all. Back up the steps, we just stood together, Claude and this dear man who would not be photographed with me. There were about four other people who had come in, so I sang the song "Next Year in Jerusalem" in Hebrew to them – they knew what I was saying. I hoped God had touched their dear hearts.

On the way back, I asked Claude to take me to another old synagogue that I had heard was in the Old City but he adamantly refused to go there. He was very afraid of being seen there. Again I urged him to go to Israel with his wife and children, and sang "Hashanah Haba'ah b'Yerushalayim" ("Next Year in Jerusalem"), at which he smiled. Maybe they did go. I certainly hope so.

Recently, I learned that the wonderful Jobar Synagogue has been totally destroyed in the Syrian war. I have seen photos – it is just a heap of rubble now. I feel heartbroken to think that this has happened. But more important is the question of the remaining Jewish people in Syria. Where are they now? Did they leave in time or did they wait too long? I just do not know.

14

The Second Unusual Tour Group – Iran

Then I Myself will gather the remnant of My flock out of all the countries where I have driven them and bring them back to their pasture...

(Jeremiah 23:3a)

It was some months after returning from Syria that the Lord began to speak to me about going to Iran. This was now 2007 when Ahmadinejad was in control and the regime was as usual threatening Israel. Christians were also being much persecuted and some in the international community suspected that schemes were under way to produce a nuclear bomb. Remembering the help we had received with aliyah from Armenia, I wondered if I could go with some of the friends from there as Iran has a small, open border with Armenia. I knew they had people going in to evangelize and also to help the Christians. Often in God's service we have our own "good ideas" but they are not necessarily God's way and this was to prove one of those times. I contacted my Armenian friend, Bagrat, by email but he was not very encouraging. He suggested I should come to Yerevan to discuss it with him. For me this would be an expensive trip, although I would have loved to see them all again. Somehow, it felt very wrong.

I sought the Lord, who made clear the reason. The Armenians look like Iranians in that they have similar features, both in hair and skin colouring. With my fair skin and light hair I would simply expose them and put them in danger. No, that was definitely not the way to go. *What then?* I wondered. The Lord showed me I was to go as a tourist and at a specific time which He would show me. It would be a "fishing" trip (looking for Jews) but also a special prayer assignment. It came to me that I should take someone with me. That was a problem as you could not have visits to Israel stamped in your passport. I was safe in this as for years I had had two passports, enabling me to visit countries unfriendly to Israel. However, from among my contacts, no one I knew was in the same position.

However, the Lord always has an answer. He also chooses exactly the right person. My friend Jean rang me with the answer. She told me, "You need someone with a brand-new passport. I thought of it because I have just renewed mine." At that very instant the Lord prompted me that she was the person to come with me! When I said so, she assured me that I had it wrong. She was 83 at that time and had problems walking any distance because of bad knees from an operation that had not worked. Definitely it could not be her. I thought the same for a brief moment, but God was assuring me that Jean was the right person. She was amazed but eventually agreed after praying and seeking the Lord.

Booking a tour of Iran was not possible from the UK so I looked online for Iranian tour groups. I found just one. It took a lot of time and prayer to arrange. A big problem was the Internet connection to Iran which was not the best. As for using the telephone, loud hissing noises, constant line breakdowns plus third-party voices shouting in the background did not help. We each had to obtain an entry visa for which we needed two copies of passport-size photos. These had to show us wearing headscarves which had to cover all our hair down to our eyebrows and be tied to the front of our chins. We completed the forms and waited. The rules of the tour dictated what we could wear, which, apart from head coverings as in the photos, included trousers with skirts covering our knees or full-length skirts, black socks, loose-fitting tops without belts but having long sleeves over our wrists. This meant that the only part of us allowed to be visible was our faces, and hands below the knuckles!

We opted for the long skirts, choosing some pretty, cotton, summer varieties which we shared and then chose from what we had ourselves. The black socks were a puzzle until we learned that toes are considered sexually exciting! The man from the tour company called me and I discovered he was in fact a lady but with the terrible phone connection it had been impossible to tell. She had arranged for us all our flight tickets, including internal flights, hotel bookings, a driver and guide. The Lord had made clear we should go to Susa (Shushan) as in the Book of Esther in the Bible. The time had come to cancel the edict made by King Artaxerxes which could not be cancelled under the law of the Medes and Persians. These laws still stood in the heavenly realm and we could see the outworkings of them today. The first edict was that all men should be masters in their households. This is still very apparent in the way Muslim women are treated, especially in the Middle East. Before setting off, Jean and I prayed through rewriting the edict to cancel it, making a new one honouring the place of women in the family.

~

With everything in place, we eventually set off in November for eight days. We had prayed that our guide would be a Christian (we knew there were quite a lot in Iran) or at least that he would be open. He was – wide open. From the start he showed a great interest in Christianity, saying it was what he wanted for himself and his wife! Everywhere we went, the people were very friendly and we were often besieged by youngsters who wanted their photos taken with us. Jean, not being able to walk far, needed to sit down frequently and rest. Because our clothes were colourful we stood out. The local people wore drab browns and greys.

Many times we would be asked questions, not only about ourselves but also about the Lord Jesus. Satellite dishes were common and people watched Western TV, including Christian programmes. We found that there were always some people who spoke English and these conveyed our side of the conversation to the others. We found that many of the Iranian people are not really Muslim, although all have to wear Muslim-style clothing and be covered up. They are really rather secular and so very open to the gospel message. The Iranian church today is growing very fast, so much so that there are many house churches, but these are being badly persecuted. Former Muslims who have become Christians can be executed, or put into prison for long spells. Many are in prison at this time.

We spent our first two days visiting museums in Teheran, which appeared an unattractive city, and then went to Shushan. We actually stood on the *Apadana* (courtyard) where Esther was permitted to speak to the king. It is one big archaeological site with just the remains of the pillars and walls. We found a spot where we could stand and cancel the edict in the Name of Jesus as Lord of Lords and King of Kings. Through the Cross we could deal with these curses. We proclaimed appropriate Scriptures and read out the rewritten edicts according to the Word of God. Then we took Communion to seal it all. It is interesting that another group from Jerusalem was sent to Teheran to do the same thing a few weeks later! Although nothing big or dramatic has happened, there is definitely now a growing movement among Muslim women for more freedom and rights. Also more and more have become believers in the Lord Jesus, which has also set them free.

We visited many different archaeological sites, one where there is the Tomb of Daniel, and also high up in the mountains, cut into the rock, were the tombs of kings, including Darius. It was all very exciting. In places Iran is very beautiful with wide rivers, colourful trees and ancient bridges. But the best was yet to come. Our guide was just the man for us. He took us to a church on the Sunday (which for Iran is a working day), but the people met at 4.30 p.m.

We were much welcomed; it was an Anglican church, started in 1938 by a British missionary, but the service was all in Farsi. Our guide listened intently and must have been greatly impacted by what he heard as, after a private talk with the pastor, he agreed to return with his wife the next Sunday to commit his life to the Lord! We heard many interesting stories from the people gathered there but their lives, it seemed, were closely watched and Muslims were not allowed to enter the church. All the same, apparently people did manage to get in. In fact one lady came enquiring while we were there.

All this gave us the boldness to ask about Jewish people. Our guide told us that there were 20,000 to 30,000 Jewish people living in Iran, mostly in Teheran, but it was impossible to identify them as everyone had to wear Muslim dress. He said he would take us to a synagogue in the town, and we were happy to accept. On arrival, we came to a gate that was just like a farm gate – five-barred and easy to open. Children were playing outside, many lovely children who wanted their photos taken, all eager and excited. And so were we! The synagogue was old and beautiful. We crept inside as a service was going on, sitting at the back with some head-covered women. We joined in as best as we could and then afterwards had a talk with them. It seemed they could perhaps leave Iran to go to Turkey or even to Cyprus, but getting permission was rare and very difficult as there was no Jewish Agency or anyone else to help them. In fact, to remain safe they had to be very quiet in all their activities. You could tell that there was an underlying element of fear in their hearts, which was true of the Christians too.

We gave money to both groups – in the church and to the leaders in the synagogue. They were touched and very grateful.

~

After this trip, which had been so significant and memorable, our guide suggested we rested the next day until lunchtime. I really protested at this since we only had a few days left. Eventually, he agreed to come at 10.30 a.m. This seemed very strange until later, when we learned the reason. When he arrived, he explained that it was "Army Day" and that there would be a huge parade in the big square where he wanted to take us. So first we went to a carpet factory and then to a shop where a man made fantastic tiny models of everything: shops, trains, castles etc. It was fascinating. At about 12.00, we finally set off for the big square as our guide said the parade would be over and it would be safe to go there. He had been worried about the soldiers who, assuming we were Americans, might have abducted us. No wonder he had wanted to start late!

The entrance to the square was a bit like a mall, with shops along one side. There were some soldiers approaching, so our guide quickly ushered us into a shop selling sweets. While we hid in there, Jean went to the "ladies". Outside, the soldiers had passed and so we ventured forth. Soon we were stopped in our tracks by some black-robed women, pointing to our feet and screaming at us and our guide. Because it was hot, we had left off the black socks and now were showing our toes – a terrible crime! Our guide was much abused for letting us out in public dressed like this. I don't think he had noticed.

Eventually we reached the huge square, only to find two enormous placards, one on each side, with giant writing on them: "DEATH TO AMERICA" and "DEATH TO ISRAEL". In between them some workmen were dismantling a high platform. All along one side of the square was a huge mosque which according to our guide was a "must see". There were many flowerbeds and at the far end a lake, such was the size of the square. However, as we walked around, Jean suddenly realized she did not have her sunglasses, an expensive pair which she needed because of the bright sun.

I have said many times that the Lord arranges everything, and this was a typical example. Nearby was a stone bench, so our guide suggested we rested there while he went to look in the places where we had been, to find these sunglasses. Hardly had he disappeared when a lady, dressed as usual in Muslim gear, came along the side where we were sitting. No one else was around. We both smiled at her because all the people had been friendly and keen to talk to us. Jean indicated to her to come and sit with us, which she did. Not sure if she were Muslim or Christian, Jean asked her, "Who do you pray to?" She whispered in French, "*Je suis Juif*" (I am Jewish). What a wonderful surprise!

It then transpired that she only spoke a few words of English. Again the Lord stepped in; my schoolgirl French of 60 years before, only occasionally used, suddenly came to the fore and so we had a conversation. Still whispering, our new friend explained that she had been a widow for eight years and had four children. Life was very hard and, more than anything, she wanted to go to Israel! Could the Lord have set it up any other way? There was I, having worked with Ebenezer, well-used to searching for Jews to go to Israel. Surely I could help her? My mind raced. I remembered that Armenia was just over the northern border. My friends there, who had helped us find Jewish people and get them to Israel, would surely know what to do. After all, some of them sometimes came to Iran.

I told her that I might be able to help but first needed to know if she had evidence that she was Jewish. "Yes, of course," she affirmed, "everything." I asked for her contact details and found a page in my notebook on which she wrote in Farsi her name, address, telephone number, etc. Not being familiar with Farsi it looked to me like hooks on a washing line, but I assured her I would do everything possible and we hugged one another. During this time no one came to the square so she was not observed. We slipped $100 into her bag when she was not looking and we said our farewells. She had just disappeared when our guide returned, having found the glasses – in the toilet of the sweet shop! It was God's perfect timing. Hallelujah! Had our guide returned sooner she might have become frightened and just left us.

We were so excited at meeting this lady and could not wait to get back to England to see how we could help. That evening we flew back to Teheran where we had one free day before leaving for

England. We went shopping near the hotel to buy chocolates, when I had a familiar nudge to go into a gentleman's clothes shop to buy a sweater for one of my sons-in-law. It proved to be another divine appointment, for the shopkeeper told us he was Jewish. He said this because apparently he thought I was Jewish. He had actually been to Tel Aviv many years before but said he simply could not go there now. He gave no explanation for this but gave us tea, making us very welcome, and even gave me a discount as I bought two of his jerseys.

The lady who arranged our tour came to see us and said she desperately wanted to be a Christian but her Muslim husband would beat her up. All she wanted was to talk about the Lord, so Jean took her privately to our room and led her in making a commitment. We learned later that she had left her husband and gone to Canada where she was safe.

~

So ended our amazing tour. But that was not really the end. Once home, after praying, I contacted Bagrat in Armenia. Like me he was excited about the Jewish lady I had met. He said I should send him the details immediately as today was Monday and they had someone going to Teheran on Wednesday. Since the note was written in Farsi, I could not email it, so decided to send it by fax. I went to our church bookshop to do so, but for some reason the fax would not go through. I tried it over and over again. Frustrated, I returned home. I had a scanner but had not used it myself and did not know what to do. The Lord clearly spoke to me: "Scan it!" I protested that I did not know what to do. Again the Lord spoke: "I do. Scan it." I put it into the printing machine and switched it on along with my computer. I cannot remember to this day what happened. I just seemed to press things and it went through! Bagrat called me to say he had received it. Then I heard nothing. Not a word for many days. In the end I called Bagrat who told me his contact had had to fly to Isfahan where the Jewish lady's family lived, find her, collect her papers and take them to the consul in Yerevan to be approved. I heard nothing for some time, expecting that Bagrat would call me. I knew that getting a visa for Israel could take time and so continued praying. Eventually, I gave in and called Bagrat who told me the whole family was now in Israel – it had taken just three weeks! He said that ten people had gone: the lady, her family, plus another married daughter and her husband, plus three children. He did not know where they were, just that they were safely in their Promised Land. Oh I was so thankful, so grateful. To this day I do not know how they got them out and Bagrat has not told me. Only the Lord knows.

~

Several months went by, when suddenly I received an email in broken English mixed with Hebrew words spelt with English letters. It was from the Iranian lady and signed "Shahnaz". She gave a phone number. How she obtained my email address I do not know. I called the number and found myself speaking to a lady in an absorption centre in Ra-anana, Israel. She spoke to me on behalf of Shahnaz and we arranged that I would visit her the next time I was in the Land. This I did and found a very happy family gradually settling in to their new life and learning Hebrew. Shahnaz, in Western-style clothes, looked ten years younger – a very attractive woman. The elder daughter had a job; the son and two other girls were at school. It was a very special event meeting them all.

After some time the older daughter married and had a baby girl. The son, Moshe, went into the army and the remaining two girls did very well in school, hoping to go to university. Shahnaz met a really nice man and as far as I know she remarried which was a big help to her. It is not easy to manage financially as a single mother in Israel. I no longer hear from the family as they left the absorption centre and I lost contact. I heard no more from Shahnaz. It is wonderful to know that our Heavenly Father made the way for them to make aliyah. He says, "Call to Me and I will answer you" (Jeremiah 33:3). He certainly does when His people really want to go home. He heard Shahnaz' cries!

15
Kaliningrad – Where No One Goes

"For behold, days are coming," declares the Lord, "when I will
restore the fortunes of My people Israel and Judah." The Lord
says, "I will also bring them back to the land that I gave to their
forefathers and they shall possess it."

(Jeremiah 30:3)

Kaliningrad? Where is that? I wondered. The Lord always arranges
things perfectly and this was no exception. I just happened to pick
up a newspaper magazine in which was an article about this region
and I wondered where it was. This was when the Lord spoke into
my heart to go there. He said that no one had gone there to help the
Jewish people. Looking through an atlas, I found it was a narrow slip
of land lying between Poland and Lithuania. From the newspaper
magazine, I learned that it had originally belonged to Germany and
the capital had been Königsberg. At the end of the Second World War,
the Russians had driven out the Germans, after which the area had
been given to them. It is separate from Russia with rail, road and air
links across Lithuania and Belarus to Moscow. Few Westerners had
been there so it remained rather isolated and little was known about
it. The article did not exactly show it to be a place for a "holiday".

A friend, Lyn, called to say she felt the Lord wanted her to come
with me so we got together to pray for dates etc. Neither of us had

contacts there, nothing and no one to help us. First we needed to obtain Russian visas; then we could book flights and, through prayer, plan our programme. The visas came with the exact dates we were allowed to go. This made eight days, which included travelling, so we only actually got six days there. We booked a hotel in Kaliningrad and another in a town towards the east called Chernyakovsk, which we could reach by rail. We felt this might be part of an aliyah highway to Moscow from where Jewish people could fly to Tel Aviv.

Our flights would take us to Hamburg from where we had booked an onward flight to Kaliningrad. There were no direct flights from the UK as very few British people went there. We packed some gifts – warm hats, scarves, gloves and socks for both children and adults as soon it would be winter and we would encounter needy people. We also had some finance to give wherever the Lord showed us – possibly to Holocaust survivors.

~

We set off in September, leaving at 5.45 a.m. for our flight to Hamburg where we had a two-hour gap before our ongoing flight; or so we thought! To our surprise, this flight was not listed on the departure board. On enquiring, we learned that the flight company, Kendall Air, had gone bust the day before! We were sent to the desk of Aeroflot, the Russian airline, where a lady told us there was no possibility of continuing on our journey that day. She booked us into a hotel, telling us that Aeroflot would fly us to Moscow and then to Kaliningrad the next day – for free, no doubt filling empty seats on their planes!

Lyn had contacts in Hamburg but thought they were travelling in Russia at that time. However, after we had sent SOS emails, we heard from one of Lyn's other friends that they were actually in Hamburg. I knew this couple but had not seen them for years. They worked with Holocaust survivors. Lyn called their home number and the wife, "E", was at home, way out in the suburbs. However, her husband, "H", just happened to be at a meeting very near our hotel! She called him and arranged for him to come and see us.

I say God sets up everything, and He really had done this. First the plane was cancelled so we went to the hotel, and now "H" was coming. Then, when we told him where we were going, he was delighted because he needed someone to go there for him to find the Jewish people! He knew of a Jewish lady whose name was Anna but he did not have a full name and address for her – just the street and a house number of which he was unsure. Also he had no flat number or telephone number. It was really very vague, but it was a start.

~

The next day was spent mainly in airports. In Hamburg we had to wait for ages before they let us on to the Moscow plane. When we arrived there, we had to wait again for a very long time before they eventually put us on a plane going to Kaliningrad. It was late in the evening when we eventually arrived in our beautiful hotel. We could see from the start that this city was not like the usual Russian places. It definitely looked German, with better-quality buildings and everything clean. We had checked online for any Jewish community and had found a street name plus a picture of a synagogue so we bought a city map in the hotel. Here again we could see the Hand of God because the hotel was just off a big main road, giving us easy access to both the synagogue and our contact, Anna, since she apparently lived along this road somewhere.

After breakfast the next morning, we set off first to find Anna's address. In Russia, a whole huge block of flats is called a "house", with the flats each being a different number. There could be a thousand families in one huge block and there are several entrances. To find the correct family one needed the house number, flat number, and entrance number or letter. Reaching the main road we tried every way we could to work out the correct numbering. Most of the buildings were large offices or businesses without any numbers.

Eventually we asked someone, who sent us in the opposite direction. We walked and walked, finally locating a building with number 12. It was at the end of the road, by a roundabout. We needed number 10, which did not seem to exist. Across the roundabout was a different road. We tried the other side of the main road, but that was no help. We asked some passers-by and they did not know either. It was very mysterious, even though I knew they understood my Russian, which wasn't good. Some of them even knew English but still we could not find the address.

Finally we decided to change tack and try to find the synagogue. Some people we met advised us to take a minibus, which we did and the driver put us off close to the street marked on our map. Again we spent fruitless time walking up and down between blocks of flats, but could not find the synagogue. We asked several people who eagerly pointed us in different directions, most of which led to churches! Tired out, we decided to return to the hotel for a rest. I was lying on my bed grumbling to the Lord because He had told us to come. To make matters worse we had arrived a day late and were to go to Chernyakovsk the next day. This only left the afternoon to do the job... Then Lyn burst into the room. "Esther, Esther, get up, we are going!" She had gone down to ask the girl at the desk if she knew of any Jewish people. She did, and through a friend had located the full address we needed, and she advised us to take a taxi, as the driver would find the house for us. Amazing!

We ordered a taxi and set off. We arrived at the end of the same road we had been at earlier. As we had done, the driver paused at the roundabout, pensively looking around. He circled it twice and then noticed a turning to the left, which went under an arch. He went in, and there, behind the main road and at right angles to it, were more blocks of typical grey, dingy Russian flats – and one block was number 10! We rang the bell for flat number 12 which we were given, and the door opened for us. A rickety old lift took us up and soon we were being welcomed by Anna and her husband, Yaakov, into a bright and cheerful apartment. We explained as best we could why we had come, using my Russian, as they knew no English. However, it was hard to understand their reply! It seemed they were both in their eighties, Holocaust survivors, who had endured both ghettos and camps. Yaakov had somehow escaped and become a partisan, but it was difficult to be sure of the entire story. They showed us photos of the loved ones they had lost. A tender relationship began between us as we hugged them, sharing their grief. They still endured the pain.

They made us some tea and then suddenly one of their sons arrived, followed very soon by one of their grandsons. Both spoke fluent English. Here again the Hand of God was evident. They were able to explain that Anna actually worked to find Holocaust survivors and to get them help. Their pensions were inadequate to pay for medicines and extras. As in Ukraine, they received about £50 a week and prices were similar to ours in the UK for many items, especially for food. We were able to tell them of friends in Hamburg who wanted to come and bring regular help. We marvelled at how God worked out the arrangements for us to meet them!

Also we were able now to tell them just why we had come and how we had tried to find the synagogue. It seemed that as a synagogue the building did not exist, in spite of the computer photo. No wonder we could not find it. Anna assured us there was one and that she could take us there and even possibly gather a few people for us to share with about making aliyah. Anna told us about those who had already gone to Israel and of some who wanted to go, but at that time no one was going soon.

We told them of our failed flight and how we were not sure about getting back to the UK, other than paying for a flight to Moscow and then on to England. It is sometimes hard to believe how God is actually in everything until it happens. The grandson told us that he had worked for the flight company that had collapsed and that he would help us to find a way back – via Poland. He switched on his computer and soon set up a route out for us via Gdansk. We could book a flight online from Gdansk with Wizz

Air – a "no frills" company like Ryan Air. "But how do we get to Gdansk?" we asked.

Apparently it was no problem. There was an early bus at 6.30 a.m. from Kaliningrad direct to Gdansk. Many people went there for the markets. It was, after all, very easy. Anna arranged to take us to the mysterious synagogue when we returned from Chernyakovsk, and so we parted with many hugs.

Chernyakovsk

The following morning saw us travelling on a train across mainly unkempt countryside, interspersed with fields of wild golden rod and through stations with pretty little flowerbeds. The route went on to Moscow and so I felt this might be a "highway" for when the Jewish people want to go to Israel. Thinking about the interruption to our journey and losing in effect two days, I had asked the Lord why. He began to show me we were in a place of identification. I did not see this until we began the return journey. We prayed and proclaimed Scriptures along the route.

Chernyakovsk proved to be a very small town with a very large hotel! I think we were their only customers. We had no contacts so we walked the streets and met many poor people, a lot of whom were sitting on the pavements, elderly people mainly, selling fruit, vegetables and small items. We gave them little gifts of warm scarves, gloves or socks, trying to tell them that Jesus loves them in Russian. We generally had a smiling response with knowing nods. During this time we were looking for anyone Jewish. We tried asking passers-by and a lady told us of one particular man and where to find him. Apparently he would be in the *Dom Kulture* – a place for cultural activities. We went there and asked for him, only to be told he had gone to collect his children from school and that we should return the next day at 10.00 a.m. This we did and he was waiting for us, surprised and curious to know why two English ladies wanted to see him! He spoke English quite well, too. We explained why we had come and he told us that the Jewish Agency was at that precise time trying to locate documents for him to go to Israel. Wonderful! He told us that his grandfather had been imprisoned by Stalin and later murdered. It was therefore likely that the family had hidden their Jewishness, which was why he had no papers. This sort of thing is very common even today.

He told us he wanted to go to Israel for the sake of his two beautiful little daughters. That said it all. Anti-Semitism was growing in his area and he could not wait to get away. He said there were a few other Jewish people in the town and he knew them. We gave him some of our aliyah leaflets with the Scriptures, which he eagerly took to give to his Jewish friends. We prayed he would be able to go to Israel very soon and that the others would also choose to go.

Taking the train back, we felt as if we were escaping somehow and realized we were identifying with the Jewish people fleeing from Russia. Returning through Poland was actually establishing, in the spirit realm, a "highway" out of Russia for a future time when we believed the Jewish people would have to flee. No wonder we felt we were escaping! We returned to Kaliningrad feeling very relaxed, and yet with a sense of adventure – surely part of the identification that we sensed.

~

We needed to book our flights back to the UK from Gdansk, but using the Internet was hopeless as it was all in Polish! There was no way we could find any information in English. We prayed and it seemed right to contact by email our travel agent in England. We hoped they would be able to deal with Wizz Air and also that they would pay for our flights until we returned. They agreed and also booked the Gdansk bus for us through their local agent in Kaliningrad. It was a wonderful answer to prayer. God is so good!

By now it was late on Saturday afternoon and we had just one day left. We contacted Anna who arranged to meet us and take us to the synagogue almost right away. Yes, the synagogue did exist, but it was in fact the main room in an apartment belonging to a dear Jewish man who greeted us at the door of what looked like a garage. There was no sign at all that this was a synagogue. No wonder we could not find it! He knew very little English but somehow we managed to converse with him. No one else came, which was not really surprising as there was some sort of festival going on in the town that evening.

Apparently approximately 20–30 people regularly attended the synagogue there. It was really the man's living room, with long wooden tables and a *bema* (podium) for the rabbi. They also had a curtain to screen off the women! I don't think they actually had their own rabbi but there was one for the region. It was probably an Orthodox group (not Ultra) meeting there. This dear man had a Yiddish name which I cannot pronounce, but no sidelocks. As it was still Shabbat, he had saved a simple meal for us, which included some *challah* (bread) from the evening before. It was a real blessing to be there.

We gave him some gifts: winter hats, gloves and scarves for the children, and for the adults scarves, warm gloves and socks. We also presented some Stars of David and little Menorah necklaces, which were most gratefully accepted. We had also brought some money for Holocaust survivors, which we gave to Anna to be used for their medicines and medical needs as she had the necessary contacts. Lastly we gave them aliyah leaflets with Scriptures and pictures to pass on to the other Jewish people. Everything was well received. I knew they had been deeply touched, as were we. It was just great to be there and hard to say goodbye. They said they would keep in touch, but we did not hear from them any more.

Yantarny

Sunday was our last day and it seemed that God had saved it especially for an important prayer action. Dear Lyn had found on the Internet the story of a most terrible event, largely unknown, that happened to the Jewish people in a little town called Yantarny, on the coast. Here most of the world's amber is mined.

Towards the end of World War Two, as the Russians were advancing, the Nazis rounded up all the remaining Jewish people from a concentration camp close to Kaliningrad. The Jews, mostly women and children, were just emaciated skeletons. They were forcibly marched about 30 miles in cold January temperatures, across bleak snow-covered ground, to this little mining town on the Baltic coast. Estimates of numbers vary between 7,000 and 13,000, and the majority perished on the way. Approximately 3,000 arrived in Yantarny. The plan had been to throw them all into one of the mining pits but the manager of the mine refused to allow it. Instead they were forced into the icy sea where they either drowned or were shot by soldiers. Only a handful escaped. The incident was covered up until 1998 when an eyewitness, Martin Bergau, who had been a boy at the time, wrote a book called *The Boy from the Amber Sea* which revealed what had happened. (I have tried unsuccessfully to find a copy.) As a result of this book, others researched the incident, culminating in the erection of a memorial on the beach in 2004.

Both Anna and the Jewish man in the synagogue had tried to tell us the story, showing us photos of the annual memorial days they hold. We knew we had to go there and pray. As we arrived in the bus the first rain of our trip began, pouring hard. We had difficulty locating the memorial, which was out of sight way down, below the cliffs. We prayed from the top overlooking the grey seas, our hearts bursting with pain. We too are Gentiles and these were God's ancient Chosen People, the "apple of His eye", driven to their deaths. The rain came down in torrents as if part of His grief. Soaked right through, we still wanted to find the actual memorial. As we walked along the road on the top of the cliffs, a car stopped. We asked the people inside if they knew where it was and, wonderfully, they offered to take us there, right down to the beach itself, via a way we had not found. This was definitely the

Hand of God. There we photographed the memorial and blessed the people. They kindly then drove us to our hotel on their way back to Kaliningrad. I felt these people must have been the Lord's provision; why else would they have stopped?

Having dried out and rested, we then went back to see our lovely Holocaust survivors, Anna and Yaakov, to say our farewells. It was truly hard to part from them. However, we knew that help would be coming from our friends in Hamburg once we passed on their details. Praise God for His way of linking people!

~

Our return home also proved to be an adventure. As we were given two different times of departure, 6.00 a.m. and 6.30 a.m., it seemed there might be two buses. Taking no chances we left early and found we were booked on the first, which was a minibus. The second one was a large coach. I have always maintained that on my travels for Him, God arranges everything. What happened next was yet one more example of this. When we arrived in Gdansk at about 11.00 a.m., our dear minibus driver said he would drive us to the airport after dropping the other passengers in the town. This would not have happened had we travelled on the coach. There was going to be a long wait for our flight and, knowing this, our driver took us for a coffee and snack in IKEA and then for a visit to the beautiful old city of Gdansk. We had a wonderful time here, enjoying the warm sunshine by the river as if we were on holiday. How God blessed us, and what a marvellous end to our trip. We flew back to Luton with Wizz Air, a very efficient airline.

We soon heard that a group from Hamburg had gone into Kaliningrad, found Anna and Yaakov, and set up a work helping Jewish people with finance, clothing and preparing their aliyah applications. By now many have gone, some of them via Warsaw, and are safely in the Promised Land. It was all God's plan and, as always with God's plan, it worked out. All He asks is our willingness to go!

16

Some of God's Timings

*'There is an appointed time for everything. And there is
a time for every event under heaven.'*

Ecclesiastes 3:1 (NASB)

When one looks at history and God's dealings with mankind there
often seem to be patterns of time that recur again and again in even
numbers. For example the Israelites were in Egypt 400 years, the
Ottoman Empire lasted 400 years from 1517 until 1917. Theodor
Herzl declared in 1897 that there would be a Jewish State within
fifty years. Fifty years later in 1947 the UN voted to establish a
Jewish State in Palestine. General Allenby took Jerusalem from the
Ottoman Turks in 1917 and fifty years later the Jews regained the
Old City in 1967.

The French town of Evian les Bains is a beautiful place, nestling
on the shore of Lac Léman, more widely known as Lake Geneva. It is
a famous holiday resort and spa town, with the Alps behind, making
it an ideal holiday resort, summer and winter for the rich and
famous. Some even made it their home, including Charlie Chaplin
and the actor James Mason. It's well-known too for its bottled water
from the springs nearby.

All this however is tarnished by the tragedy for the Jewish
people of Europe that unfolded there in July 1938. Representatives

of thirty-two nations gathered at the Hotel Royal to discuss and try and solve the Jewish refugee problem unfolding in Europe. Although every nation's representative expressed sympathy, nearly all, including Britain and the USA, said that they were unable to take any refugees. Hitler realized he could do what he wanted with the Jews; as his spies told him, "You can do as you like, because nobody cares."

Fifty years later in 1988, God sought a response. Representatives of forty-four nations came together, first in Berlin and then in Evian, to humble themselves before God and repent in deep shame for what their nations had done many years before.

Some 2000-3000 people went to the conference, among them 700 from the UK and I was one of them. Each country appointed a representative to stand on the platform in Berlin and confess the sin of their nation. I will never forget that moment when our delegate went and confessed Britain's sin. We were standing in complete silence and I saw in my spirit a huge eye which examined my innermost being. It was totally awesome.

It had been fifty years since Evian and forty years since the rebirth of the State of Israel. It was a significant time for certain.

The conference became significant for me too. While I was there the Lord began to impress on my spirit the outline for the route of a journey He wanted me to make. Shaped like a trumpet the route took me from one side of the Soviet Union to the other and back.

Back in Israel I was contacted by a lady called Helen Mears who began a ministry called *Streams in the Desert* – it provided homes in Israel for elderly *olim* (new immigrants). She had heard about my proposed trip and said she felt God was telling her to accompany me. I felt this was right and together we sought direction as to the purpose of the trip. It turned out to be another period of training in hearing and obeying the Lord's instructions!

The Lord showed us that we were to take gifts for certain people, mainly clothes. There were to be four sets. One was a travelling set for a man who might be on a journey. Another set was for a young woman, another for a one year-old boy and the last set was for a baby. We had no idea who these individuals were, but knew that God would point them out when the time came. That much I knew from making other journeys appointed by the Lord!

In our minds Helen and I thought the men's clothes might actually be for the missing Swedish diplomat, Raoul Wallenberg, who had saved thousands of Jews during the war by providing them with Swedish passports. The Soviets had arrested him and he'd never been seen since. At that time there had been much in the news about his disappearance and reports that he might have escaped.

We initially attempted to set up the trip through the Soviet travel agency, 'Intourist', but realised this wasn't right when it became very complicated and they said they'd 'lost' our papers!

Then we found what seemed to be the ideal tour. Going from Leningrad to Khabarovsk and back, partly flying and partly on the Trans-Siberian Railway, it stopped at cities in Siberia and ended in Moscow. The route fitted the trumpet shape I had seen in my vision and, as it was a pre-organised tour by the travel company, it was easy to book ourselves on it.

Soviet Union

The time came to depart and it wasn't long before we were looking round Leningrad (now St Petersburg) doing all the usual tourist things. We then caught a long internal flight right across Russia to Khabarovsk in the Soviet Far East, next to the border with China. It is only when you fly across Russia that you realise how vast this country is. You're on a plane for hours and hours, passing through different time zones and yet you're still within the same country – amazing!

We arrived in Khabarovsk and felt that the Lord was saying we would find the young woman to whom we should give the clothes in a church.

That morning our group was taken on an excursion around the city and Helen and I noticed a small orthodox church. We carefully took note of the route back to the hotel.

We excused ourselves from the afternoon excursion to a museum as we were tired so, after a rest in the hotel, we set off to find the church we had seen.

There was a service in progress, with not many people attending and those who were there were standing, which was customary. There was no young woman among the worshippers.

We found a bench at the back and sat down. It wasn't long before, to our joy, a young woman came in. She joined in with the prayers and I went and stood beside her. I held out a Bible for her to see which she gazed at in astonishment. Indicating for her to come to the back I led her to where Helen was sat with the clothes we had. They were just the right size! The Lord is so amazing. The young woman was overwhelmed and radiant with joy at receiving them and the Bible. We couldn't communicate with her verbally so indicated with signs that the gifts were from the Lord Himself.

As we left I found myself asking God, "Why her, Lord?" I felt Him say that she had been crying out to Him for her people and that He wanted to comfort her. God is good.

From Khabarovsk we continued our journey on the Trans-Siberian Railway. This was an interesting experience. The scenery was quite beautiful although at times we noticed labour camps with thin ragged people working in them – a legacy of the infamous *gulag*.

At many of the stations on the way to our next stop at Irkutsk there were peasant women selling handmade goods and food on the platform. We weren't however allowed off the train. In fact our group was in the most expensive compartments and had our meals before anyone else and so it was exceedingly difficult to have contact with the other passengers, let alone people on the platforms.

At Irkutsk we were taken to a hotel near to a village called Listvyanka on Lake Baikal, the largest and deepest lake in the world. There was an excursion in the morning which comprised a boat trip on the lake and a tour round the village. In the afternoon we were given some free time. Both Helen and I felt that here we would find the one year-old baby boy that we had to give the clothes to.

A dusty road circled the small village of primitive wooden houses. We followed this road, keeping an eye open for signs of a baby boy. Some children were wheeling a baby sitting up in a large old pram but it was too young to be the one we were looking for. The children asked for chewing gum and had obviously encountered tourists before.

I asked the Lord for help, for a sign and then suddenly noticed through a fence a child's pushchair. Excitedly I pointed it out to Helen and as I did so we were spotted by a lady inside the house. She opened the gate and I pointed to the pushchair and made the movement of rocking a child with my arms. She invited us to sit on a wooden bench and we showed her the clothes we had. It wasn't a surprise to us that she did indeed have a little boy about a year old. She was as excited as we were and seemed very grateful. Although we couldn't communicate in Russian we smiled and pointed upwards indicating that the gifts were from God.

Outside we noticed that there was no red, wooden star on her house and wondered if it meant she was not a communist. Could she have been a believer that God was blessing? We had to leave that question with Him.

Our next stop was Bratsk, a town where a river had been dammed to make a huge hydro-electric power station. We were told it had been built by volunteers but of course we knew that such things had often been built by slave labour.

There was a terrible atmosphere in the hotel and indeed in the town where a drug and alcohol problem with attending violence was evident. There was no church.

We lay down on the floor in our hotel room, praying. The Lord showed us we were to take communion and then put the wine into the water by the dam when we went there the next day. We felt that God wanted to bring spiritual cleansing to this site. We knew that on projects like this the slave labour was terribly abused and many people would have undoubtedly lost their lives in its construction.

The next day our group was taken to see the dam. It was indeed impressive and we watched the huge volume of water pouring through, driving the turbines. There were high iron railings keeping us away from the water and we wondered how we would get near enough to pour in the wine. I had the bottle hidden in my bag.

When we were taken to the top to see the turbines, the noise was so loud that Helen and I sang boldly, "Jesus is Lord." No one heard us except the Lord Himself!

Back outside, as we went down the steps, I heard myself ask the guide, who was a KGB agent, "Can we go right inside by the water to take photos; it is so beautiful?" He thought for a moment and then went off to fetch a key to the gate.

We all went through and Helen began to adjust the settings on her camera to take some pictures. Everyone was looking at the foaming water so I slipped to the back of the group and surreptitiously poured wine into my hands and let it drip through my fingers into the water. It stained the foam red as if the blood of Jesus was being spilled for those that had perished in such terrible circumstances. I was very afraid and my heart was pounding lest it should be noticed, but the group seemed to be engrossed in giving Helen advice over her camera as it had jammed and they hadn't seen what I had done. God is so good. When He wants us to do something, He makes a way. He just wants us to step out in faith and do it. All my fears melted – I was so relieved.

We found out later that others had been that way too and prayed. A wonderful answer to those prayers was that eventually a church formed in the town and subsequently an office of Ebenezer Operation Exodus opened to assist in finding Jewish people who wanted to go to Israel. Hallelujah!

We flew to Moscow, our last stop. We did the usual tourist thing, visiting various sites and making the most of 'shopping' time by visiting the Baptist Church. Here there was always a service on and as usual the place was packed.

We were sent upstairs and, when we reached our seats, I suddenly noticed that the woman next to me was pregnant. We still had the set of clothes we had brought for a baby. In the semi-darkness of the dimly lit church I nudged the woman and showed her the baby clothes I had brought. She was dumbstruck, taking the little clothes, fingering them and feeling the quality. Such things were difficult for ordinary people to afford in the Soviet Union. She showed them to the people next to her, marvelling at this 'miracle' she had been given. We were thrilled too. What a great God we serve!

All we had left now was the set of clothes for a man on a journey. Was it likely that they were for Raoul Wallenberg? It seemed unlikely. Helen and I prayed together and decided we should go to the big synagogue in Moscow.

We arrived and found a service taking place. As we were shown up to the ladies' gallery, we could see the men down below with their prayer shawls around their shoulders, praying. To my great delight I saw the man I had met on my previous visit to the synagogue. He had been outside then, looking thin and gaunt as if he had just been released from prison. Now he looked very different; fit and well. I had given him a Hebrew Bible before and wondered now if he had read it and found his Messiah.

We sat down and I put my bag under my seat, glancing at the woman next to me. I suddenly felt a warmth come over me and I realized that this woman was the one to whom we should give the last set of clothes. We were once again in exactly the right place at the right time. I whispered to Helen and we both smiled at the woman. She couldn't speak English but when we showed her the clothes her face lit up as if she knew exactly who they were for. We handed them over to her, joyfully trusting that God would get them to the person for whom they were intended. Could it be Raoul Wallenburg, we wondered? (In truth he was never found and probably died in a Soviet prison camp somewhere).

Poland and Berlin

We returned to England and the Lord told me to go to London the very next day to make preparations for another trip; this time to Poland. I had no money left but in obedience to the Lord's instructions went to London and booked the train to Warsaw via Berlin. After returning home I discovered that inexplicably there was indeed money in my account. How it got there I have no idea. However, I still didn't have any to take to people in need. The Lord then reminded me that I had some jewellery. I hadn't up to then felt that He wanted me to sell it but now knew that I should use it for this trip so I would have something to give.

It was late September, Poland had just become free from their Soviet overlord but people were poor. There were many old folk with hardly enough to live on, who would struggle to pay their heating bills in the harsh Polish winter. Ten English pounds at that time would be enough to pay the heating bills for someone right through to spring.

My friend in Poland took me to all those she knew who had either survived the holocaust or been involved in rescuing Jewish people. I saw people buying a quarter of a loaf of bread or one potato. It was all they could afford. They were suffering and it was a joy to be able to help them, bringing the reality of God's love with some practical assistance, showing He had not forgotten them.

I stopped in Berlin on the way home and my friend there took me to a place where an artificial hill had been made from the rubble piled up after the wartime bombing. My friend went there alternate Sundays to pray.

From this hill one could see right over the Berlin Wall, beyond three fences, guard dogs and the armed soldiers on guard. Often my friend would wave at the guards she could see without getting any acknowledgement. However, she said that on the last occasion she waved and one of the guards waved back albeit surreptitiously! "Something is happening," she said. "Things are changing!"

There was a bench on the hill and we had brought a newspaper to put on the damp seat to sit on. However God told us to roll the newspaper and make two 'trumpets'. It was now 1989 and it had been fifty years since the beginning of the Second World War. God wanted us to declare the Year of Jubilee, (a year of liberty mentioned in Leviticus 25:10) and 'blow' into our 'trumpets' north, south, east and west. We proclaimed a Scripture over the infamous Berlin Wall that had divided not only the city but had kept families split up for years. We then 'blew' our 'trumpets' making the sound as we did so. It was quite awesome. The route of our journey had been shaped like a trumpet and this action seemed to complete in the spirit realm what we had done in the natural realm.

Two weeks later we heard that the Wall had been breached. Hundreds of people had gone to the Wall on the west side of Berlin to pray. They walked along it, painted Scripture verses on it and one group from a church had apparently been every week to place their hands on one particular large brick to pray for it to come down. When the wall was breached this brick was the first to fall out! What an awesome God we serve!

There had been seventy years of communism, fifty years since the war and forty years of a divided Berlin. I felt there was certainly something significant about these timings.

17

More Adventures in the Former Soviet Union

First a journey to Ukraine

We eventually made three visits to Chukotka, with a period of a few years between the second and third trip. During this time the Lord gave us plenty to do, with both Hannah and I going on prayer journeys, sometimes together and on other occasions independently.

One trip I did on my own was in the summer of 2001 when I went with Helen Mears as her prayer partner to visit aged potential *olim* who needed a place in which to live in Israel. Helen had established a very important work called *Streams in the Desert*. This provided homes for elderly Jewish people, some of whom were Holocaust survivors. They had no relatives and no other help in Israel and found settling in the land both expensive and extremely difficult. They could not learn the language, manage the money, cope with the climate and much more. Some who had gone were found living on the streets, sleeping rough. Understandably the Israeli Consuls became increasingly reluctant to give visas to single, elderly Jewish people, unless they had somewhere to go and someone to help them. Many of the people Helen helped didn't need to be in a care home – they were still active and independent. They just needed to be somewhere they could afford and where they could be with others like themselves. Giving them an invitation to live in their own room in a specific house meant they should be able to get their visas.

Helen, through *Streams in the Desert*, had set up four such homes in Beit Shemesh, but she needed to meet possible candidates and also talk with the Jewish Agency leaders and the Consul in Kiev so that they understood what she was offering the people. So I went with her to Ukraine. We were to visit people in three towns – Odessa, Kiev and Kharkov. We visited the Consul and the Jewish Agency first where Helen was able to explain the purpose of our visit as well as show a beautifully illustrated book of photos demonstrating the reality of the houses. It is one thing to send faxes and emails but much better to meet people face to face. Everyone was impressed and we were well received everywhere. In fact the Jewish Agency rep in Kharkov was so impressed that we had come so far that he took us out to lunch and loaned us a car and driver for our visits!

The really special part of the journey for me was to meet some of the needy elderly people. I had travelled far and wide in the work of "fishing" for Jewish people to go to Israel. I had seen many poor homes, but this time I saw some of the poorest yet. Some homes were hardly more than sheds with a long walk to fetch water. What they did for washing and toilet facilities we dared not ask. With no proper heating – usually just a hotplate near the floor (which was very dangerous) – they faced very cold winters and, with little lighting, the places were dark and dismal.

Inside we found dear old souls who had survived the Holocaust, still lost and alone, struggling to live with no one to help them. How they existed we did not know. To prepare to go to Israel was too difficult for them to comprehend ... and they were afraid! As Helen spoke to them and showed photos of the homes in Israel, we saw hope coming into their eyes. We spoke of God's promises and read some of the Scriptures telling of His call to return. We handed out a Star of David necklaces, putting them round their tired old necks. Even this little gesture helped as they began to feel really Jewish, and wept tears which we couldn't help doing too. Some told us they wanted to go to Israel, whilst others were very wary. However, we gave their details to the Ebenezer teams to follow up. We heard later that one of these elderly souls was making *aliyah* on the very next Ebenezer sailing from Odessa to Haifa, while others were preparing their documents.

It was a real privilege to meet these dear folk and to share from our hearts what God was preparing for them. Many did get to Israel and some went to stay in Beit Shemesh. *Streams in the Desert* is currently in the process of preparing a Triage Home to cover more aspects of care for the elderly. More information on this important work can be found by contacting: streams@ streamsinthedesert.org.uk.

Next an unexpected trip to Germany

I had hardly returned to England when I received a request from a friend in Germany called Uta. She had looked after me on my first journey to the former Soviet Union (see chapter 2 of *The Ingathering of Israel*). She was a paediatrician and a very sweet lady who has since gone to be with the Lord. We became great friends and she often visited me in England and sometimes went to Israel. Her family had lived in East Germany but had managed to get to the part of West Berlin where she worked. However, after the collapse of communism the family received back their property in East Germany. When Uta retired she went to live close to Altenburg, near to the family home. She did not actually live in the property as it was huge and had been divided into flats which were all let. Instead, she rented a small apartment in a village nearby.

In no time I was flying to Leipzig because Uta had invited me to celebrate *Rosh Hashanna* (the Jewish New Year) with some Jewish people who had left Russia for Germany. I knew this to be direct from the Lord and you couldn't have prevented me from going. However, I was astonished when I arrived. Everything was grey – in Leipzig and Altenburg and everywhere in-between. I remembered how drab East Berlin had appeared when I had gone there. This was even worse. Everything was run-down and in need of repair. Nothing had been done in all the years that the Russians had occupied the country. If you leave a shed or garden fence for a long time, it will turn grey. This is what had happened to all the buildings – houses, flats, shops, stations, offices ... everything. It was so depressing. Some people had managed to find paint and had begun the work of restoration, giving a bit of colour here and there, but it was limited. They really needed a lot of help as most people were still very poor.

We had a very busy week visiting many of these newly arrived people in their homes. They proudly showed us around the very nice flats the German government had provided and furnished for them. We were told the government wanted to rebuild their Jewish communities, lost in the Holocaust, so they were encouraging Jewish people to come from Russia instead of going to Israel. With all that was provided, many were arriving each day. They were being taught German and given money until they were ready for jobs. They were, without exception, very pleased with their new lives. As always we found they knew almost nothing about being Jewish or why they ought to be going to Israel so they had no desire to go there. Germany seemed a much better option! Personally I was appalled and very saddened.

The *Rosh Hashanna* celebration proved very special. Many gathered, invited from the surrounding area, arriving in mini buses and cars. We had a time of singing Jewish songs and then the leader, Peter, who spoke Russian, told them of God's special love for them and how they were the chosen people of God for whom God has a special purpose. They eagerly drank in everything. We served them food – tasty fish or chicken portions, with chips, salads, crusty bread etc followed by very delicious gateaux. Then I was asked to show slides of the *aliyah* from the fSU. They saw how we looked after the people as they arrived, how they were cared for in the bases, and then their life on-board the ship and their arrival in Haifa. Included were beautiful photos of Israel; the mountains in the north, the beaches and the fields of fruit. It was meant to encourage them to make *aliyah* themselves. However, within seconds most of the guests were sitting with their backs to the screen and deliberately talking among themselves, drowning out what I was saying. I was shocked at their reaction. I tried to quieten them but then one man stood up, very angry with me, and shouted that they wanted to stay in Germany, that this was their new home and that I should go away and leave them alone. There was a chorus of agreement – no one wanted to watch the slides. They were all, without exception, annoyed that I dared to try to persuade them to go to Israel!

These Jewish people gave every possible reason for staying in Germany even though anti-Semitism was prevalent in that very city. Even in Leipzig, where I had been at a prayer meeting, we had suddenly heard a shout and police sirens. "It's the neo-Nazis, again," explained my friends. "We often get this." I was in the area for only eight days yet, during that time, the same groups caused trouble in the town of Buchenwald and damaged a synagogue in Dusseldorf. Here in Altenburg, every evening I heard loud shouts, drums being banged, fireworks and lots of noise as a long group of pro-Nazi youth paraded through the centre of the city shouting about "Germany for the Germans" and demanding that foreigners get out. The Jewish people protested that the German government would deal with it, it would come to nothing and they were safe there. The disturbances in Israel at that time did not help either. They would not be persuaded. They did not sense the danger they could be facing and in fact did not want to face it.

The good thing was that Uta, Peter and the team were there to help them learn about being Jewish. They could answer their questions about why they were chosen and teach them from the *Tanakh* about Jewish customs, keeping the Sabbath and the feasts. They also taught them some Hebrew and Jewish cookery – so many things to awaken their Jewish hearts. Seventy years of communism had taken its toll. They had not been allowed to practise their own faith and so for most it had died. Maybe in time some would go for a tour in Israel. God wants them there and, in teaching them from the Scriptures, He will awaken their hearts. This we believed and began to pray for. It was an eye-opening trip for me and I still trust God to move on their hearts in His own way for He said, "I will bring them ..."

A call to Kazakhstan – a demonstration of God's love

It was later in November 2000, when Helen Mears from *Streams in the Desert* received a fax in perfect copperplate English handwriting that told of an elderly man in Kazakhstan who wanted to go to Israel. The local Ebenezer team had put the Jewish community in touch with *Streams in the Desert* to see if they could help him since he was alone, with no family. Helen needed to be sure that he was fit enough to look after himself and had a list of what people needed to be able to do. As she was unable to go and meet him, I felt the Lord wanting me to make the journey. It was a privilege from start to finish.

It was to be a long journey as I had to go via Moscow where I stayed overnight with the Ebenezer leaders there. I set off from the UK on November 14th and the next day flew on to Almaty in the south of Kazakhstan. En route to the airport I was more and more astonished at the changes in Moscow. It now looked like any other western capital with bright lights and too much traffic. Then suddenly the taxi hit a large rock in the road, causing the vehicle to rock about and zigzag dangerously across the busy road. As I cried out the Name of Jesus, it miraculously became steady again, coming to a stop without colliding with other traffic and sustaining only a split tyre! Russian drivers are very adept and after quickly putting on the spare we were on our way again within a few minutes. Praise God. It really could have been a nasty accident.

The flight to Almaty in Kazakhstan usually takes four and a half hours. Both Aeroflot and Kazakhstan Airlines had new, up-to-date planes that were clean and comfortable, and the food was good. We were soon served breakfast. Much of the country is like a desert and uninhabited. The time passed quickly as I prayed and dozed. Eventually we started the descent through heavy clouds to the city of Almaty but heard the weather was too bad for us to land so we turned back north towards Karaganda. Two hours later we landed at Astana, the new capital of Kazakhstan. Approaching the runway, it was only too obvious that it was covered in snow and ice from the recent blizzard. I called upon the Lord for the safety of this plane full of people. For a fleeting moment, He allowed me to see a host of angelic beings seemingly bearing the plane up on their wings. They gently landed it with scarcely a bump! What a glorious Lord we serve.

Inside the airport a small bar offered tea and coffee, our first refreshment since the breakfast we had enjoyed some five hours previously. We waited and waited. Two hours later an announcement told us we were flying on to Almaty! The Ebenezer team had arranged to meet me but, as I did not have a mobile phone, I could not let them know about the delay. A very kind young German lady helped me call the Moscow office so they could pass on a message. We eventually reached Almaty fourteen hours after leaving Moscow, arriving at about 2.00 a.m. The two young EEF leaders were still there waiting, all cheerful with a great warm welcome and I was soon fed and settled in a hotel room for the rest of the night.

The next morning we met to discuss the situation and I was introduced to the team. They were doing a marvellous job under conditions we could not imagine in comfortable Britain. We had lunch and then set off for a flight to Petropavlovsk in the north, right on the border with Russia, near to Omsk. (There is another Petropavlovsk, in Kamchatka, which should not be confused with this one.) A dear brother called Andrei (a volunteer) was assigned to travel with me as my interpreter. It soon transpired that he knew very little English so my Russian was about to receive a big brush-up with the aid of a dictionary. The small plane was very old, with steps up under the body and entry similar to getting into a loft! It held about 20 people and there was no seat allocation so it was a case of first on, first served! We were told the flight would take about four hours; the only refreshments were plastic beakers of mineral water which tasted a bit fishy. We did not go up very high and the plane was very noisy due to its age.

After about three hours, bad weather meant we had to land at a small remote airport in a place called Kokshetay. Inside the airport there was no heating, food or drinks and stone floors without seats. Thankfully there was a toilet, but only one for everybody, behind a large chipped enamel screen and illuminated by a dingy light. A ramp up dirty steps, held four holes with 'mud' all around each one – no doors, no water, nothing. It was a communal facility but there was no choice. Afterwards I had to go and clean my boots outside in the snow where the temperature was –20 °C but it felt colder inside!

After much waiting, getting colder and hungrier, it was decided to send us on by taxi. Of course this took a long time to arrange. We were told the journey would take about two hours but we just wanted to get on our way.

Eventually we set off, four to a taxi with three in the back and one beside the driver. It was pitch black out there but at least we were sitting down and we got warm again. The snow and ice blanketed the roads including the many potholes. Thus we bumped through the night, dozing intermittently en route. There were no service stations or cafés, nothing it seemed for miles and miles through the dark forests. We stopped after about three hours to drop off the two other passengers in the forest. Although it was totally dark, they seemed to know where to go! Then about an hour later we saw the lights of Petropavlovsk. At last!

Of course as we approached our journey's end the taxi driver asked for an address – but Andrei didn't have one. I was appalled. How could we come all this way and not know where to go? Thankfully Andrei said he had the telephone number of a pastor who was expecting us and was going to help us find the Jewish man we'd come to see. So we stopped in deep snow, to call him. There was no answer. We waited and tried three times. There was still no reply. Then I remembered: before I left England, the Lord had prompted me to take the original fax with me. At the time, I could not see that this was necessary, but HE knew. I found it and, praise God, it had the phone number for the Jewish leader. When we called we spoke to his wife who told us that, although he was out, he would be back very soon. Eventually we learned that the pastor who was expecting us lived in the same block of flats as the Jewish leader. We got the address and were able to return to our patient taxi driver.

When we arrived at the block of flats we found that the pastor and his wife had returned, having been waiting for us at the airport! When they'd been told that we were travelling the final stretch by taxi, they'd returned home. The Lord is amazing at the way He times everything and sorts things out. It was nearly midnight but before long, with Pastor Nikolai and his wife, Natasha, we were tucking into pasta and "something", but at least it was warm! They had arranged beds for us yet it was obvious they were quite poor. These people will give all they have, as we had found before.

The next day was the highlight of the trip. Everyone seemed to know everyone else. We were taken down to meet the Jewish leader and his wife and then we set off for a short walk in the snow (about a foot deep) in freezing temperatures of −20 °C, to the home of the man we had come to see, Alexander Steinberg. It was my task to meet this dear old man and to assess the situation. He was so delighted that I had come, he just hugged and hugged me. He was a retired neurologist who also wrote poetry and painted in oils. He had never married and was alone in the world. Mercury poisoning in the atmosphere had affected his heart and lungs so he urgently needed to go to Israel. He had a very small, modest home of one room, with tiny kitchen and bathroom, typical of the provision of the fSU.

How much the Lord loves him, I thought, as he told us about his illnesses and how he longed to be in Israel. We soon completed the papers for I found he could manage all that was required of him so I was able, there and then, to give him the required invitation to a home in Bet Shemesh. He was so excited, having waited a long time.

Then the Jewish leader invited us to the Community Centre for afternoon tea! It transpired that the local council – if that's what it was – had allocated all groups a place where they could meet. In the case of the Jewish community it was one long room, rather like an elongated sitting room. After lunch with the pastor and his wife, we were taken there to meet what proved to be most of the local Jews – about 12 of them, all seated around a long narrow table. They had arranged a tea especially for us, little cakes, some sweets and small fruits. It all looked very pretty. We were welcomed in and offered cups of Russian tea as they apologised for having no vodka! Russian tea is very different from ours, weak, sweetened and without milk. It was very refreshing. They wanted to thank us for coming, me in particular, as it was truly a long journey. This meant that the leader made a long speech, complete with a toast, which was mostly beyond my ability in Russian. A lady nearby, whispered the translation for me. Then they wanted me to give a speech, also with a toast, which I felt obliged to do, saying how much we cared for them and were grateful for all that the Jewish people had given us, and how we owed them a great debt. I went on to ask their forgiveness for what Christians had done to them down the centuries and how ashamed many of us were. They just wanted to wave it all aside, hugging me and shedding a few tears, which I did too.

Because of the influence of communism they claimed to be atheists, so how could I expect them to believe in God? Nevertheless, with passages from Scripture, evidence in creation, examples from the work of *aliyah*, it was not long before you could see hope rising in their eyes. God certainly started a work in the room that day! Later we prayed they would seek Him and start to read their Bibles (the *Tanakh*) and find Him for themselves.

I mentioned to the lady translating about the beautifully written fax we had received and it proved to have been from her! Then she surprised me for she said, "It is you who got all the rest of my family to Israel!" I could not understand as this was my first visit to Kazakhstan. What could she mean? She went on to explain how her father was Edvard Zilberstein from Leninaken, in Armenia. He was the man with a wife who had twice fallen and broken both of her hips as she tried to get water from a stand-pipe outside their home. They lived under the remains of a tower block which had collapsed in the Armenian earthquake. He also had a disabled son with cerebral palsy, plus another son and a daughter. I remembered now that he had told me of another daughter who had married and gone abroad – and here she was!! Ebenezer had helped the whole family to go to Israel. The story is in my first book *The Ingathering of Israel*.

I was amazed at the way God sets things up. She told me how the family love Israel, are very happy there and that she, together with her husband and daughters, were planning to make *aliyah* very soon. Then she introduced me to two very beautiful young teenaged girls seated nearby – her daughters. What a great joy rose in my heart.

The next day, we flew back to Almaty without any hitches, where the temperature of –6 °C seemed warm after –20 °C, plus it was sunny. That evening we began the next adventure, which I had not expected. It started with a 14 hour overnight train journey to Shymkent on the border of Uzbekistan. It was very hot and noisy on the train. We had top bunks and, with the bumping and shaking, had little opportunity for sleep. Neither could we wash or change so I had to sleep in my clothes.

Somewhat rumpled and weary, we arrived at 8.10 a.m. the next morning to be met by Dimitri, the Jewish leader. He had asked Ebenezer to send me there. He took us to the Jewish Cultural Centre, which consisted of two adjoining flats that were being renovated. The power was off, the water was cold, and there was nowhere in all the rubble where we could get washed and changed. However, they had prepared a breakfast of coffee with bread and jam. It was most welcome after the dirty train.

Dimitri, it transpired, had heard of my coming on behalf of *Streams* and had asked that I come and visit people who might also be eligible for living in the homes available in Israel. We spent the day visiting a number of Jewish people who were wanting to make *aliyah* but for couldn't for various reasons. In the first home, we met Rosa and Violetta, mother and daughter. Rosa had had an operation on her back which had left her totally bed-ridden, unable to sit or stand. Violetta could not walk more than a few steps with sticks. It was heart-breaking for them, trying to cope. Obviously they were not suitable candidates for *Streams* so who, I wondered, could help them? They needed another source of help and I promised to try and find one. (This I did later when in Israel but I never did hear if they ever got there.)

We next visited Emily, a cheerful chatty lady with a small dog who seemed to want to bite me. She would easily fit in at Beit Shemesh when a room was available. How desperately more housing was needed for these people! It took a long time to do the interviews as they all wanted to chat and soon it was lunchtime. The Jewish group had prepared a splendid meal during which time they asked all about Ebenezer, the ship from Odessa and life in Israel. It was a very special time, after which we hugged and hugged each other.

We then took a taxi far out of the town to visit a couple called Tanya and Mikhail. They really did want to go to Israel but had nowhere to go. They were both well and able to look after each other – the main problem was that they could not sell their flat. (I am not surprised really for it was far outside the city, small, in need of much repair and the couple were asking too much). We agreed on a three-month hold on a room in Beit Shemesh, hoping they would go to Israel without selling their flat especially since they would not get much for it.

We returned to the Centre and discussed others needing help but there wasn't time to visit more. The next taxi to the station had

200

me praying since the driver cut in and out between other vehicles, narrowly avoiding collisions and deep potholes, which he skirted with the edge of his wheels. The taxi, which appeared to be an ancient vehicle, was kept going by the unusual technique of pushing the choke in and out whilst pumping the clutch up and down. I thought the car itself would fall to pieces at the rate he was driving.

And so back to Almaty on the train – another 14 hours, all hot and dirty. It was wonderful to reach the hotel for a shower and a change of clothes the next morning. That day we had time to pray together and hear updates on the work in Kazakhstan. Then in the evening, a group of *olim* was leaving to fly direct to Tel Aviv. The team had been gathering them over the last few days from many areas and now they were in the same hotel as us where they were to celebrate with a farewell party. Ebenezer had started this idea when we first had the ship sailings from Odessa and now each base did the same. It was a wonderful time for both them and us. It was such a blessing to sit with them as they heard God's Word about their return to Israel and the volunteers sang Jewish songs. Before long the buses came and their luggage was loaded on board. I noticed that their possessions were packed in the ubiquitous strong, striped nylon bags, a big change from those used by the first *olim* years before. I remembered how back then their possessions were done up in old curtains, often a faded shade of green, and tied around with string! There were no labels either and often they all looked alike. We had had to put named sticky tags on each so their owners would eventually be able to identify their own. Waving them off touched my heart as I saw God's Word being fulfilled before my eyes.

The next day I flew back to Moscow where it was –20 °C, but then on to my warm cosy house in England. I kept thinking about those precious people and the situations in which they lived and worked. However there was much to be thankful for and I could praise God for all that had been achieved, realising how much He loves His people and sending me on that long journey initially to find one old man who wanted to go to Israel. And he got there!

Back to the Arctic

Whilst Hannah and I were in Chukotka for our last visit in summer 2001 our pastor friend Sasha had told us that he originated from Norilsk. We discovered this city to be far west of Chukotka but still within the Arctic Circle, 2500 km northeast of Moscow. Sasha said that his sister, Luba, still lived there and would like us to go and visit her. It seemed there was a small new church which was struggling to survive. Would we go and pray with them?

Sasha told us that the region had been one of Stalin's worst death camp with the majority of prisoners Jews and Christians, but mainly Jews. The conditions had been appalling, beyond imagination and thousands had died. Their bodies had been mostly buried where they worked in the construction of factories, roads, towns, mines and the airport. Raw materials such as coal, gold, copper and iron-ore had been found there which was why the prison camps had been set up. Sasha said that the survivors had had no choice but to stay in the area when the camps had closed after Stalin's death and they were now very old and poor. The mining had continued, presumably with slave labour but they had not been worked to death as before. However, eventually the mines had closed at the end of the communist era. Then much later, a consortium of Jewish entrepreneurs had bought the mines, restored them, and were now operating them, employing many, many people for salaries three times they could earn in Moscow. People were very willing to go there just for the extra money in spite of the Arctic conditions.

Sasha showed us photos of Norilsk, which he explained was dark throughout the winter and light throughout the summer. In the photos we saw brightly lit streets, modern cars and big shops where it was possible to buy anything, even fresh fruit and vegetables! How could this be in this Arctic part of Russia? He thought it was great that the city was fully lit 24 hours a day in the winter by bright street lights and so was never dark. He said the people were wealthy and had a good time! They apparently worked shifts of 12 hours on and 12 hours off for three days and then had three full days off. What could they do in their spare time, I wondered? It transpired they had similar amenities to elsewhere in the 'western' world – cinemas, theatres, sports halls, swimming pools, skating rinks, football and rugby pitches; virtually anything one could think of. Outdoors there was skiing and hunting. There seemed to be plenty to do. Also with 12 hour shifts and little natural distinction between day and night you went to bed or got up when you pleased. It all sounded a bit strange and far-fetched to us. But we understood there were still Jewish people there – a lot apparently. Also the church was struggling. We knew we should go.

It was November 2001 when we went. We knew it would be dark and cold but it was the time the Lord said to go. Luba had arranged everything for us in Norilsk and booked us into a hotel. Unfortunately, although our flight via Moscow was direct to Norilsk, we were diverted to a small airport "somewhere" because of bad weather. However, we weren't told this and so, when we landed, we naturally thought we were at Norilsk and were puzzled by the lack of personnel and the non-appearance of our luggage! The other passengers did not seem perturbed as we all sat in an unheated waiting room, just waiting and waiting. All was very quiet with no one to tell us anything.

After a while we began to think we had got off at the wrong place and the plane had gone on without us. With my little Russian, I tried to find out and very helpful people tried to explain to us just what was happening. We did not understand. No one knew English except for a few words, even a child tried to help with school type English. Then quite out of the blue, a man in a brown tweed suit appeared as if from nowhere and came to tell us the situation. There had been a blizzard which was not uncommon and we would be delayed for about four hours. His English was perfect. How he knew about us, or where he came from we could not tell for we did not see him again. Was he an angel or airport staff (we had seen no one as yet) or was he another passenger? We could only guess. Personally I think he was an angel as I had had such experiences before.

The four-hour delay had us arriving at 1.30 a.m. the next morning, to be greeted by dear Luba and her friend Natasha, still waiting, all love and big smiles in their vast fur hats and coats. Luba, the sister of our dear friend Sasha in Anadyr, looked exactly like him! We loved each other on sight. We were whisked away by taxi to a very smart, modern, clean hotel where we spent the rest of the night getting some much-needed sleep. Typical Brits, we were up to have breakfast by 9.00 a.m. and then waited for Luba to come. She didn't. We waited and waited, then tried to call her. When she eventually answered she expressed surprise that we were up so early as she was still in bed. We soon learned that time was a very different and uncertain factor in Norilsk. With all the lights on in winter and constant daylight in summer, there seemed to be no night or day. What a topsy-turvy world it was to us.

At about midday, Luba arrived complete with thick warm Russian hats and long fur gloves for us to put over our English versions. Later she also loaned us thick fur capes to go over our very inadequate coats. Then we were taken by taxi to Sasha's old flat which they had set up for us. People from the church had prepared much food, filling the fridge and cupboard. There was more than we needed. They had also arranged taxis for us so that we did not get too cold walking. We were so well cared for and cosseted, showered with love for coming so far to help them. It seemed they had been praying for Western Christians to come and pray with them about their difficult situation and here we were.

We set off to meet the team of Christians that had gathered and they explained about their problem. How should they deal with the spiritual oppression that seemed to cover the area? A hard spiritual darkness seemed to pervade the atmosphere, which was not surprising given the awful history of the city. It seemed to be a spiritual version of the oppressive physical situation of ten months of winter, with terrible cold, blizzards, fog and bitter winds etc.

They said it was less cold than usual when we were there, –15 °C to –20 °C. Bad enough, we thought! It was snowing most of the time, with snowploughs constantly clearing the roads. Behind the town the snow was piled higher than any buildings, many of which were tower blocks, because it never melted. And it was dark for nearly the whole day. The sun came up far away on the horizon at about midday – a pink ball just tinting the sky and the dirty snow and then it went down again within a few minutes. That was all the 'daylight' we had. What a place to live!

They explained to us that there were four towns, all built by slave labour in the time of Stalin, around the mining area now known as the *Kombinat* which means factory zone. The furthest east was called Talnach, then came Norilsk. The *Kombinat* was in the centre and past that westwards was Kiyerkan and then much further on was the port of Dudinka. A railway line had been built to Dudinka taking mined goods to be delivered elsewhere by ship. The actual factory area was swathed in thick smoke given off by the chimneys, enveloping that region in a strange fog and making it look unworldly, like some sort of 'never-never-land'.

They also explained how the factory area was a vast zone where Russian managers were employed to oversee the shifts, twenty four hours, seven days a week. People were paid a lot of money to work there. For example, a truck driver earned $1000 a month compared with the more normal $150-$200 for the same job elsewhere. In Moscow you had to have three jobs to earn $800 which you needed in order to survive. The workers only did three 12 hour shifts a week so had plenty of free time to enjoy themselves. However there was much alcoholism, drug taking, prostitution and crime.

It was no wonder the churches were struggling with few coming to faith. The people were wealthy, life was good – who needed Jesus? Only those with serious family problems such as mothers with teenagers on drugs or wives with alcoholic husbands (the usual problems in the fSU) would think of coming to church to seek help from God. Often people did not stay. Older people including

Christians who had survived the camps, now in poor health and living in poverty, would turn to the church for help which was gladly given. Usually these folk were too frail or disabled to actually get to church meetings. The problems seemed endless. No wonder the churches were small and people discouraged.

Then we asked about the Jewish people and were told it seemed nearly impossible to move them. They formed two different groups – those who had come there to work and those who had survived the camps. Those who chose to work there and had wealth were not interested in going to Israel. Why would they when they lived in luxury in Norilsk? That was their thinking and response. Those who had survived the camps were very old and poor. No one cared for them and they were too frail to think of moving. Also, they had no documents to prove their Jewishness, most having been destroyed in efforts to hide themselves as Russians, to avoid further pain and persecution. Neither had they any other relatives to help prove their ethnicity, they just knew they were Jewish and nothing more. To assist any that did want help there was a small Ebenezer team in Talnach, and someone as a representative in Dudinka.

There was much to pray about so we got before the Lord. He led us to arrange our days so we visited each town for prayer, did warfare with proclamations and tried to meet people to encourage them and pass on the gifts we had brought with us. In preparation we prayed, listed proclamations to use and looked up addresses so that Luba could contact folk to say we would be visiting. Then we hired a six-seater vehicle to enable us to travel freely from town to town starting the next day.

We set off early, first reaching the area of the Kombinat. It was amazing. Thick smoke poured out of high chimneys, giving off a strange warmth which caused a fog to form. Everything was enveloped. It was a vast area of huge factory buildings, with the sound of machinery working non-stop and people going about clad in thick overalls. We were glad when we had got through it and reached the other side. Next we drove past Kiyerkan, which looked like quite a neat small town, and then we came to what I can only describe as a white desert. It was just snow, but grey and bleak and it stretched away for miles, flat and uninteresting. We did see a white fox – well that is what we thought it was and later a large white animal like a dog but not near enough to identify it properly.

Dudinka surprised us. Far away from the *Kombinat*, it looked bright and clean. The buildings were all painted pastel shades which actually looked quite pretty except that they were not in particularly good repair as were the buildings in Norilsk. There were a few shops, well stocked with food, clothing, shoes etc, much better than towns elsewhere in Russia. We soon found the flat we were to visit and received a great welcome from Olga who was waiting for us. As always, there was a meal ready, with hot coffee which was just what we needed. Soon we were down to work to discuss the situation there and to pray with her. It was really much the same as in Norilsk. The church was very small and there were a few Jewish people working in the port who had no thought of going to Israel. They too had good jobs! However, Olga wasn't discouraged because the men listened to what she said and were happy to take the Scriptures she handed out. Also, when she managed to speak with their wives, they appeared more interested, which is why she remained hopeful.

We went for a walk to pray around the dock area and some of the streets, using our proclamations as we went. Then it was time to set off back. We called in at Kiyerkan to meet with some Christians and a pastor there. This town was smaller, really quite homely and clean and the houses well built. There were no vast blocks of flats as there were in Norilsk. However the same problems with preaching the Gospel existed. The people were basically too well off and comfortable to realise they needed the Lord! Any Jewish people living in this neat, tidy town were employed in the *Kombinat* or other businesses and could not be persuaded to even think about going to live in Israel. We prayed with these dear people and left them some brochures about Israel to give to the Jewish people. We returned to Norilsk, once more traversing the fog-enveloped area of the *Kombinat*. We were relieved to be back and able to spend the evening with Luba who showed us many photos of her family, especially of Sasha when he was young – a very handsome youth!

The next day we drove to Talnach to visit Angela, the Ebenezer representative and her two helpers. They were feeling rather down and needed encouragement. We got the impression they thought we'd come to criticise them for the lack of Jewish people going to Israel which of course was far from the truth. We listened to their stories, assuring them that we fully understood. We actually did not know of anywhere else where it was so hard even just to live, let alone try to help the Jewish people decide to make *aliyah*. They knew and helped many very old folk; not just Jews as this caused jealousy and anti-semitism. They told us some of their stories. One very old lady, now very disabled, had been taken from Moscow where she had been an opera singer. No reason was given other than the fact that she was Jewish. She had been made to work down a mine using a primitive type of scoop to dig out soil in order to deepen the shaft. She told how she was down there for long hours in a squatting position. The food was poor and in small amounts and she had been sexually abused regularly. It was amazing she survived. They told us how she weeps even today, as she has never really recovered. They said this story was typical. We prayed with them about the whole set up and as we had some financial gifts to share we were able to give them a substantial amount to help these dear old people. This did a lot to cheer them and we left on good terms.

Then we had to get our packing done because after church the next day we would begin our journey back to Moscow and the UK.

It was a special treat to worship together with the believers in this town so far away within the Arctic Circle. We prayed with them and together repeated the proclamations we had made in the town, sealing it all with the breaking of bread.

Parting was difficult as we were leaving these dear people coping with the situation but they were very grateful that the Lord had sent us in answer to their prayers for help. We've had little news since because very soon after our visit, tourists were forbidden to visit. It seemed the area was the worst in all of Russia for crime, drug taking, alcoholism and prostitution and the authorities did not want foreigners to go there anymore.

Landing in Moscow, we changed planes and then were held up for three hours because of a blizzard which almost buried us. We just sat in the plane and watched. It was amazing – as soon as the blizzard cleared, out came some huge snow-ploughs to clear the run-ways. They were the width of the tarmac so it was soon done. Meanwhile, what looked like machines with enormous hair-dryers, blew the snow off the planes! They did one plane at a time and it was a bit like sitting in a car wash when they did ours. We were very impressed. It took time to clear all the delayed flights but at last it was our turn and soon we were en route for Heathrow and home. We arrived back very grateful to the Lord for sending us to such a place and giving us more insight into how to pray for its people. Another adventure over.

Hannah and I made a number of different spiritual warfare/ prayer journeys across Russia from the Far East right to Leningrad, including one that involved crossing the whole of Russia from Khabarovsk to Leningrad in three stages. On this trip we were able to visit the more remote Ebenezer bases, meet the leaders, and hear about their situations. These journeys did not involve finding Jews, but were more a case of encouraging, taking gifts and getting facts again helping us to pray more effectively for them all. However, this was our last trip together to find Jewish people and to work with the Ebenezer teams in bringing them back to Israel. It was after this that the Lord spoke to me – that I should go to the nations, and He meant to the four corners of the earth.

18

Some Far East Trips

North Korea

Having returned from the Far South East (Singapore, Australia and New Zealand) I was next led by the Lord to go to countries in the East (North Korea, Cambodia and Vietnam) on two separate trips.

Going to North Korea proved to be the toughest assignment, spiritually and emotionally, that I had ever had and my heart ached from what we saw and heard. We did not find any Jewish people there and could not make contact with any of the people, let alone speak to believers. Some Christians are so secret and hidden that there was no way to contact them. I know today that brave Chinese and South Korean Christians do get in with help and the underground church is growing. However, anyone, and I mean anyone, suspected of deviating from the Party line is incarcerated in a camp along with their entire family. There is no religious freedom whatsoever. The regime runs political labour camps where many thousands of people are held. Tens of thousands are Christians facing torture, starvation and death. Children and adults are kicked to death, gassed, executed and even experimented upon with chemicals which are later used for making weapons. We heard of Christian children put into cages and hung in trees, left to die. Had there been any Jewish people there they'd have been killed off long ago, unless they escaped during the Korean War.

As a nation, North Korea has long been closed to outsiders, a secretive giant Gulag of some 20 million people. It has become one of the poorest nations on earth, frozen in a time warp because of its isolationist policies. Then some years ago they had some serious crop failures when people starved to death and refugees began sneaking over the borders, risking their lives to cross rivers and get into China. Word got out that a 'crack' had appeared in the system and that teams could go in as 'friends' of the country. Of course we were shown a lot of 'great achievements', all the benefits of living in such a wonderful country. There were squares with monuments, museums, an art gallery, a women's hospital, a children's palace and much more, everything attributed to the original leader, Kim Il-Sung. Although he was now dead, he was considered a god, and known as the 'Eternal Leader', always with them. Then came his son, the Great Leader, treated as 'god the son'. The religion was known as *Juche* (the spirit) and it mocked the Trinity. The people were brainwashed into this – except for those who truly knew the Lord.

We were kept totally separate from the native population, in a hotel on an island with guards, and in a bus for our visits. At least we could see for ourselves – the streets almost empty of cars, no old people (they had died of hunger), no buggies for the little children who were carried on backs of their mothers and there were soldiers everywhere. We saw people, all very thin, gathering grass and tree bark (presumably to eat), walking for miles (there were no buses for them), working in the fields, harvesting maize and rice by hand. Some were even shifting banks of earth by hand using plastic bowls! This earth was being used to make bricks from the mud, which were left to dry in the sunshine. There was poverty everywhere. At night it was pitch dark, no lights whatsoever except those illuminating the statues and memorials of the 'Great Leader' – there were floodlights for him!

What about God's Chosen people who were said to be scattered into *all* the nations – were there some here? Very circumspectly I asked the guide: "Were there people of other nations – as we have in our country? Russians, Chinese?"

"A few maybe", he acknowledged.

I pressed him a littler further, "What about wandering people like say – er – Arabs or Jews?"

His response was instant. He looked me straight in the eyes and said, "No Jews! No, definitely no Jews!" He was so very positive, I felt his reaction to be strange but could not tell why as he said no more and just turned away. I thought about it – perhaps there had been some and they had escaped during the Korean War, or had all been killed because of their religion? In any case, although I had watched the crowds, I had not seen anyone looking Jewish.

We could not speak to the people and we certainly did not find any Jews. However, I did have opportunities to talk with the other members of the group, to tell them of God's plans for His people and some were interested. As a group we had prayed and prayed, quietly so as not to be noticed. We worshipped softly and proclaimed His Word as we drove around the country. God had sent us there. I certainly had been directed to go, so we trusted Him that in His time, He would set these dear people free.

Cambodia

Within a month I was off to Singapore and then to Phnom Penh, capital of Cambodia. From there I would go on to Ho Chi Min City (formerly Saigon) in Vietnam. The aim was to encourage the believers in both countries, to talk to them about Israel and God's plans and purposes for His people, and of course to seek out any Jewish people in both countries.

Cambodia was recovering from the Pol Pot regime when more than one third of the population perished. Although poor, the people were very friendly and cheerful. They travelled on small motorcycles called *motos* and also used them as taxis. Whole families (even up to seven people) would sit on one vehicle, the women riding sidesaddle. Of course I had to use one quite often, even aged 73 as I was then! It was a bit hair raising since drivers turned right or left with no signals, and everyone weaved in and out a bit like dodgem cars! A bigger vehicle was called a *tuk-tuk* which is still a moto but with a chariot on the back. It had four seats and a striped plastic awning to cover it - quite fun for getting around!

Christianity had only been accepted a few years ago and so the churches were very small. I spoke with the pastor of one, telling him of God's plans for Israel. He was very dismissive, feeling he had more important things to think about. I was taken to a big hall where they had a meeting for local pastors. About twelve elderly men were on the stage, faces shining like they had been polished. They were survivors of the Pol Pot regime, and had been imprisoned and tortured for their faith. Praise God for such precious men. Some of the believers I met at this meeting were interested in what I had to say and told me they too were seeking Jewish people in the country. However, even after two or three years, they had not found any. No one, it seemed, knew of any. It was thought that they had either left during the time of Pol Pot, or had perished at that time. The story was very much similar to that in North Korea, except that now these dear Cambodian people were free once more.

Vietnam

In Vietnam the country had recovered much more than Cambodia and was in fact doing well on the tourist front. In some ways it was similar with hundreds of *motos* and *tuk-tuks*, but here there were also *rick-shaws* and *cyclos* – larger bikes with a basket-type seat on the front on which a passenger could sit. By the end of our visit we'd used them all.

I was able to meet with a group bringing materials in for the believers who are constantly harassed, beaten up, and imprisoned although the Communist Vietnam Government asserts otherwise. We met some from the house churches. This had to be done very carefully and secretly for they are watched closely and can be picked up at any time and thrown into jail. Their houses are ransacked, items stolen etc, yet you would never think so to meet them. They were all smiles and totally bold, telling us stories, quietly and humbly, about their daily lives.

When we asked them about Jewish people they assured us there were lots in the city and had no doubt about it. They had been celebrating *Hanukkah* we were told. This encouraged me very much. However, later, we discovered that the Jewish people in Ho Chi Min City were in fact visiting businessmen and doctors who had come to help! Probably they were Israelis who were typically out to advise and help in such countries.

We walked through a shopping mall and a huge market watching for anyone looking Jewish, praying for the Lord to reveal them to us. Like the Cambodians, the Vietnamese are petite in build with straight black hair and almond shaped eyes. No one looked Jewish and it seemed that, as in North Korea and Cambodia, any Jewish people had either escaped or been killed during the Vietnam War.

When we learned of an Israeli Embassy, we checked the address in the Yellow Pages and then set off to find it. As we wandered around trying to decipher the street names, two eager drivers on *cyclos* assured us they knew the whereabouts of the Israeli Embassy – only ten minutes away they said. We each sat in a basket-type seat on the front and the two cyclist drivers set of wobbling about among the motos and tuk-tuks in quite a precarious way leaving us feeling a bit vulnerable to say the least, perched as we were at the front! Soon we arrived, only to find it was the Australian Embassy! Next, some minutes later it was the British Embassy, then the American Embassy. We did not want any of these and we kept repeating that it was the Israeli Embassy we were looking for. Nearly an hour later, we stopped to ask someone and were told that it was not in Ho Chi Min City at all! Rather it was in Hanoi – way, way to the north of the country and too far to go.

We had had a grand tour of the city in all the dust and weaving traffic, costing a lot in dollars, before finally they agreed to return us to our hotel. We needed a good bath and change of clothes as we were covered in dust!

We had certainly tried to find Jewish people and for me it was three countries where there seemed to be none. Besides that there had been no real chance to teach the people of God's plans and purposes for Israel. All I knew was that the Lord sent me and I had learned to watch, listen closely to discern if any were in fact Jewish and to make the most of any opportunities to talk to people about Israel.

Another aspect of the trip was that we visited other ministries. The main one was on an island in the Mekong river which we reached by leaving at 5.00 a.m. to take a *tuk-tuk* to the river and then a long ferry ride to reach this remote place. A couple from Australia lived there and cared for over 1,200 to 1,700 children, mostly orphans, some street children, ragged, barefoot and dirty. They gathered together each day, children from about 2 years old and upwards to sing and be told stories before they each received a packet of food before they left again. Many had AIDS to which they had lost their parents but I remember their brown eyes filled with hope as they lined up for their parcels.

The couple held a church service later when many adults arrived at their large wooden hut on stilts. The group I was with had items to help this couple as well as finance. It was a privilege to be with them. Coming home to the run up to Christmas and the New Year was hard after all I had witnessed.

So ended my trips to the northern part of the Far East. Where next I wondered?

Epilogue –
The Ingathering Goes On

On November 29th 2018, my mother Esther Lever died. Her death was instantaneous and completely unexpected. It was recorded as a cardiac arrest. She was 86 years old and at the very moment of her death, in a geriatric hospital near Tel Aviv, praying for the elderly father of her dear friend Yossi. She was attended by several Israeli medics who were unable to resuscitate her. Her visit to Israel had been to take photographs for her third book which teaches about how the land and the city of Jerusalem are inextricably linked to the Lord's plans and purposes. This was to be my mother's final journey of service and adventure.

On December 19th, 2018 she was buried in Beersheba in the Alternative Cemetery. The funeral service was gloriously joyful and her final resting place can best be described as heavenly, overlooking the desert and facing towards Jerusalem. Her death, funeral and burial were all in accordance with the Lord's perfect will, a reward for her years of service and dedication.

It is perfectly fitting that she should die and be buried in the land of Israel, but above all in Beersheba. When the Bible speaks of Israel's borders it uses the phrase "from Dan to Beersheba." It is a place which is intrinsic to the beginning of the Jewish people's claim to the Land.

Abraham, the father of the Jewish people dug a well there. It was taken by Abimelech but Abraham contended with him for its return. It was returned and the two made a covenant concerning the land Genesis 21 v 31: So that place was called Beersheba and the two men swore an oath there. Beersheba is the first place to which Abraham laid claim. In the twentieth century, General Allenby, himself a devout Christian, led his troops in victory against all the odds over the Ottoman forces in the Battle of Beersheba – an event which would lead to the restoration of the Jewish people to the land.

The last almost forty years of my mother's life were spent in service to the Lord, working to restore the Jewish people to their spiritual homeland, this land which was first laid claim to by Abraham in Beersheba. She was utterly uncompromising in the way she followed her call to help with the final Aliyah and to teach the truth of the scriptures regarding God's plans for His people and His land. This book "The Ingathering Goes On" is testament to this. She literally went to the ends of the earth.

In the early days of her calling to leave the UK to in Israel, my mother was given the scripture from Ruth 1 v 16 -17:

"Entreat me not to leave you, or to return from following after you: for wherever you go, I will go: and wherever you lodge, I will lodge. Your people shall be my people and your God, my God. Where you die, will I die and there will I be buried."

These words are on her gravestone in the cemetery in Beersheba and are a magnificent testimony to God's faithfulness.

My mother was a truly remarkable person of faith and action. I pray that her books which describe her many exploits continue to inspire and bless everyone who reads them.

Angela Oakley
April 2021

About the Author

Esther Lever (1932–2018) is perhaps best described as a modern-day warrior, tirelessly and relentlessly battling to find the far flung, forgotten Jewish people and urge them to make Aliyah to their spiritual home. Many of her breath-taking exploits are described in this re-release of her second book "Israel, the Ingathering Goes On."

Hers was a life of resolute faith encapsulated in the words of Ruth 1 v 16 -17 "Don't urge me to leave you or to turn back from you. Where you go, I will go, where you stay, I will stay. Your people will be my people, your God my God. Where you die, I will die and there I will be buried."

She travelled to "the ends of the earth" following her calling, from the Artic wastes of Kamchatka in the Former Soviet Union and other parts of Russia, Germany, Ukraine, Tibet, China, India, Burma, Cambodia, Vietnam, North Korea, Iran, and Syria. Every chapter bears testimony to the faithfulness of God and the fulfilment of His word which takes place in plain sight.

Esther Lever was one of those extraordinary people one meets perhaps once or twice in a lifetime; people who impact one's life in a way that is inspiring and thrilling and cause us to yearn for a deeper walk with God.

The Ingathering of Israel
A Life Called to Miraculously Help Jewish People Return to Their Homeland
By Esther Lever

We never know what amazing adventures God has in store for us as we respond in obedience to His calling. Flying in old Russian helicopters and planes in a war zone, sleeping under kitchen tables, and dodging shadowy figures that were following her – would all seem a long way away from Esther's ordinary life lived in England, especially at an age most retire to a quiet life. But when God calls someone to something as dramatic as helping Jewish people return to Israel from the remote regions of the former Soviet Union, miracles are never far away.

Divine intervention, angelic help and God moving in power are all part of this inspiring, even courageous story of how Esther used the latter part of her life to help bring Jewish people back to Israel in fulfilment of Biblical prophecy. Throughout this book you will come to know how God can speak dramatically into any person's life and take them into places one could never imagine. It is also a story of God's passion to keep his ancient word to His people, the Jews.

"Esther had a determination to be obedient to her Lord, and because of this God has been able to use her as a support to Jewish people in many remote parts of the earth. She has been travelling the world in search of Jewish communities would say that Esther is pretty remarkable herself.

To enable her to fulfil her calling, God has intervened many times in supernatural ways and sometimes by angelic visitations. The stories of the people and events she describes make inspirational reading.

I certainly think she is for her willingness to put up with danger, discomfort, and problems at an age when most of us are looking to put our feet up and take it easy.

It has been my privilege to know Esther for some years now. I know her motive for writing this book is not to attract attention to herself. It is rather to respond to God's prompting to write it in order to show that He has in no way cast aside the Jewish people but on the contrary has much yet to fulfil in His purposes for them.

If you have an interest at all in Israel and the Jewish people, you will enjoy this book." - *Russell Bowles*

ISBN 9781852407100 • 176 pages

Why pray for Israel

Whilst the world's critical attention is focused on the conflict raging within and around Israel, this book will inspire you to be part of God's plans for Israel and the Church.

"What makes this book so unusual is the fact that is not just an emphasis on the fulfilment of divine prophecy, adding to our Biblical knowledge, but is a challenge to be involved, and it become intercessors and prayer warriors for Israel."
- *Lance Lambert*

ISBN 9781852405052 · 320 pages

Homecoming, Our Return to Biblical Roots

This book encourages us to interpret the New Testament through the filter of the Old just as the early apostles had done. It will provide solid foundations for understanding the roots of our faith in the Hebraic past.

ISBN 9781852404673 · 300 pages

Israel, Land of God's promise

Israel is the most misunderstood nation on the planet. The Jewish people are the most consistently persecuted in all of history – ancient and modern – why? Can the Church afford to pursue its historically notorious treatment of the Jew and the nation of Israel? The author compels us to examine Church history and Jewish history in the light of God's Word.

"Murray Dixon helps us understand that the destiny of the world today, including the Church, and the destiny of Israel are closely woven together."
- *Hugh Kitson*, Author and documentary film-maker

ISBN 9781852407353 · 228 pages

Sovereign World Ltd
Bringing together the Word & the Spirit

Please visit our online shop to browse our range of titles.
www.sovereignworld.com
or write to the company at the headquarters address:

Sovereign World Ltd.
Ellel Grange
Bay Horse
Lancaster
Lancashire LA2 0HN
United Kingdom

Or email us at:
info@sovereignworld.com

*Most books are also available in e-book format
and can be purchased online.*

Would You Join With Us To Bless the Nations?

At the Sovereign World Trust, our mandate and passion is to send books, like the one you've just read, to *faithful leaders who can equip others* (2 Tim 2:2).

The 'Good News' is that in all of the poorest nations we reach, the Kingdom of God is growing in an accelerated way but, to further this Great Commission work, the Pastors and Leaders in these countries need good teaching resources in order to provide sound Biblical doctrine to their flock, their future generations and especially new converts.

If you could donate a copy of this or other titles from Sovereign World Ltd, you will be helping to supply much-needed resources to Pastors and Leaders in many countries.

Contact us for more information on (+44)(0)1732 851150 or visit our website www.sovereignworldtrust.org.uk

> *"I have all it takes to further my studies. Sovereign is making it all possible for me"*
>
> **Rev. Akfred Keyas – Kenya**

> *"My ministry is rising up gradually since I have been teaching people from these books"*
>
> **Pastor John Obaseki – Nigeria**